Ten (& More) Interesting Uses for Your Home Computer

by Tina Berke

Editing by Cynthia Collier and Gretchen Lingham
Cover illustration by Randy Verougstraete
Inside illustrations by Lisa Mozzini
Art direction by Kay Thorogood

First Edition Copyright© 1990
Computer Publishing Enterprises
P.O. Box 23478
San Diego, CA 92123

0-945776-08-X

ACKNOWLEDGEMENTS

I am greatly indebted to the following people: Mom, Jack, Gret, Wally, Scott, Jan, Andy, and Dan—and all my family and friends who have patiently held my hand during the writing of this book (although it did make it harder to type). Thank you.

My thanks also to all the various computer software publishers and distributors who kindly sent me copies of their terrific programs. The world of computer software is an exciting one, always full of suprises, and always an education.

Tina Berke
September, 1989   San Diego

To the readers, staff, and founders
of *ComputorEdge* Magazine,
without whom the word "work"
would just mean "job."

CONTENTS

APPENDICES

FOREWORD

Why don't more people buy computers? If you've used a computer, or better, if you own one, then you know how useful they can be. A computer can help you become more productive, educate your kids, assist you in your mental chores, and entertain you. Yet, two thirds of those who can afford a PC don't buy one. Why?

The answer will surprise you. Basically, people don't know what the computer can do for them. Those people need this book. And if you think you know everything a computer is capable of, then you need this book as well.

Conventional thinking really tends to pigeonhole the things a computer can do. People limit their ideas about computers to numbers, equations, programming, word processing, or playing silly games with pretty graphics and loud, annoying sounds. But the computer isn't the scientist's or "computer nerd's" plaything any more.

This book was written because, sooner or later, just about everyone will get into computers. They attract users from all walks of life. And from those walks, people have learned to train the computer beast to do certain tricks special to them. So on the edge of the giant word processing-spreadsheet-database soup bowl you have programs for gardening, health food, and the accult, as well as a myriad of other useful computer applications you would have never thought available for your machine.

Some would say this stuff is weird. I disagree. Instead, it's a few flowers on the edge of the desert—a doorway into an entirely new world for the computer. Open this book and take a peek into that world. Learn some new tricks to teach your computer. And in the end, hopefully, you'll discover why no one really buys a computer—they *invest* in one.

Dan Gookin,
January, 1990

PREFACE

One day when I received some gardening software from the UPS guy in preparation for an article for *ComputorEdge* Magazine, the looks of surprise on some of the computer "veterans'" faces around the office prompted me to wonder how many other different, non-business uses for computers existed.

This book is the product of many months of exploring the sometimes offbeat, always adventurous "other" side of computing.

T.B.

September, 1989   San Diego

INTRODUCTION

Has your home computer become just another appliance? Do you find yourself using it more for work, and not for fun? Does it sit hulking in your spare room, taunting you to work, work, work? Do you dread sitting down at your computer only to scroll through yet another spreadsheet, text file, or database entry? Or have you hesitated to buy a computer because you have no need for dry, boring business applications like databases, spreadsheets, or word processors?

If the answer to any of these questions is "yes," or if you're just curious about new uses for your home computer, you need this book.

The number and variety of personal computer software applications is boggling, once you start looking. I've looked at lots of software, in many categories, and have tried to break down home software into ten different families. Instead of talking about specific packages in detail, the book talks about goals you want to achieve and the types of software that will help you achieve them.

The book is written in plain English, without a lot of technical jargon to weigh you down. You can read it front to back, or just skip around to the sections that look most appealing. An index will help you with a specific need. You'll find appendices in the back that explain CD-ROM software and hardware, and tell you how to get up and going with shareware programs.

In the back of each chapter you'll find a detailed list of software sources, but don't stop there. Software publishers have only started recognizing the need for home applications. New software titles appear daily, so keep looking: Somewhere out there is a package that will do what you need it to do.

Chapter 8, The Learning Tool: Educational Software, focuses more on the ways adults and whole families can use their computer for learning. For a thorough look at the best (and worst) in child-oriented educational software and hardware, take a look at Computer Publishing Enterprises' *Parent's Guide to Educational Software and Computers.*

Remember, personal computers were designed to be tools for fun and education, as well as productivity. This book can be your guide to getting more uses out of your computer than you ever thought possible.

PART ONE

CHAPTER 1

Household Applications

There your computer sits, hogging up space in your house. If your spouse were sitting around so idly you'd probably put him or her to work. Why not make your computer pull its weight around the house, too, by letting it organize you where you need it most? Although it can't take out the garbage, it can help in ways you probably never dreamed possible. Best of all, it can save you money and give you more time to lounge idly too!

If your heating costs are telling you that your money's going up in smoke, your computer's ability to crunch numbers can show you where to cut energy expenditures. There's even a program to calculate how much wood a wood-burning stove uses up. (But it won't be able to tell you how much wood a woodchuck chucks...)

Homeowner's insurance is essential. Yet tracking everything you own can be tedious and time-consuming. Let your computer log in your possessions in case you ever need to replace them. Home inventory software is good insurance in itself. Just be sure to keep a copy of the home inventory data diskette off the premises.

If holidays are for relaxing, why are there always so many last-minute details to see to? With the right software, your computer can do everything from play holiday tunes to print greeting cards. And it won't hog up all the Christmas cookies while it's doing so, either.

Once the holidays are over, you'll probably want to give the house a good cleaning. If rearranging furniture is about the most unpleasant task you can think of, let your computer do it for you. Although they're not very strong, computers can set it all down on a grid so you can see what looks good where, before any muscles come into play.

Your computer can design and print unlimited calendars and labels. Now you can print out a calendar for each member of the family with specialized dates, like birthdays, highlighted.

This is the only nation on the planet where companies offer you money to try out their products. But saving coupons is often seen as a time-wasting hassle. Your computer can organize those coupons and rebates for you, letting you save money with ease.

TASKS FOR HOUSEHOLD APPLICATIONS SOFTWARE

- Charting Home Energy Costs
- Logging Home Inventories
- Helping Out Around the Holidays
- Moving Furniture
- Designing and Printing Calendars and Labels
- Organizing and Tracking Manufacturer's Coupons

CHARTING HOME ENERGY COSTS

Your computer can save you money by telling you how much you're spending to heat your house. *Home Utility Recorder* for the IBM/Compatible family of computers asks you to enter in your monthly utility bills. The program averages the cost, and gives you a detailed analysis of where your energy dollars are going.

After looking over the computer's report, you may decide to add solar panels as a source of energy. A program called *Telisolar* will help determine the cost effectiveness of such a project. Any remodeling projects you then decide on will be based on intelligent comparison.

If you decide that a remodeling project's for you, a program called *Homeowner* will organize the renovation and save you money. Don't rely solely on the contractor's figures. Let your computer be your remodeling consultant.

HOME INVENTORY/HOUSEHOLD RECORDS SOFTWARE

You know you should get organized and record serial numbers, etc. of all your possessions. But the task seems too tedious. Don't wait until a fire or theft makes conducting a household inventory impossible. *Homeventory* for the IBM/Compatible family of computers is typical of a type of software that lets you easily create an inventory of your home and its contents. The program comes with rooms already defined, plus ones you can customize to meet the configuration of your own house. For the items in each room you enter descriptions, prices, purchase date, serial numbers or other identification. You then get a detailed list of your valuables, either for insurance records or just to gloat over how much neat stuff you've accumulated.

```
        ******  Add an Item  ******  (To exit, enter blanks, choose M )

          Residence: John Q. Public
            Address: 123 Main St., Anytown, USA
               Room: Living Room
              Item #:  1
  *** Type ONLY within [ ] brackets ***   Press Enter for next field
        Description: [Stereo                            ]
      Purchase Date: [12/25/89] mm/dd/yy
     Purchase Price: [2,500.00   ]  dddddd.cc
    Place Purchased: [Wow Stereo                        ]
      Serial Number: [123423                ]
          Other I.D.: [                                 ]
        Other Info 1: [                                 ]
        Other Info 2: [                                 ]
```

Figure 1: Household inventory programs keep records of your possessions.

Most of these programs let you add, revise or delete several times later, in order to keep everything current. You can print out the inventory room by room or once for the whole house.You and your computer will enjoy recording all your possessions together.

HOLIDAY APPLICATIONS

When spirits are high and everyone's having fun, why not involve your computer in the festivities? Programs for your computer can play holiday sounds, print cards and holiday letters, or teach you and your family more about a holiday's meaning and origin.

For Apple and IBM computers, programs from Davka in the *All About* series feature comprehensive guides to customs and practices of Chanukah, Passover, Purim, and other holy days. *Christmas Sampler* from Cross Educational Software illustrates "The Night Before Christmas" and "The Christmas Story," and plays 12 carols. Another program from the same publisher called *Christmas Story* teaches the Bible version of Christ's birth.

INTERIOR DECORATOR/PLANNING SOFTWARE

What if your computer could help you plan a furniture-rearranging sessions before a single piano was lifted? Many software packages exist to save you some sweat, by showing you just what that new arrangement you're considering will look like.

Floorplan, for the Apple family of computers, assists you by drawing a room from input you give on room size and shape, location of doors and windows, and other details. From the IBM/Compatibles shareware family, *Magic Mover* performs a similar function. And *BDL.Move* was designed to help your possessions survive either an office or home move without too much trauma.

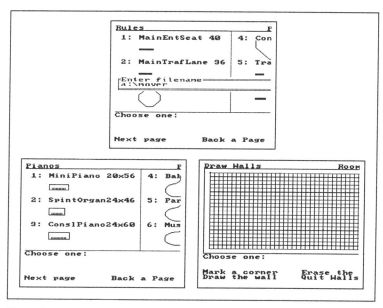

Figure 2: *Furniture-moving with a computer saves your back.*

LABEL MAKERS/CALENDAR PROGRAMS

You'll have to search for the disk labels again—or any kind of label, for that matter. Equipped with label-maker software, your home computer can identify everything you own: video tapes, files, nametags, and more. Most label-making software lets you specify the dimensions of the label you want, along with type sizes and orientation. You can print multiple copies of a label just by pressing one key with *Labels Unlimited*'s "ditto" feature. This program also lets you print sequentially-numbered labels—good for inventory and archive purposes. And the computer's ability to print neat graphics will enable you to better read those labels.

Even though this is the age of the paperless home office, sometimes a wall calendar still comes in handy. But as they fill up with duties and appointments, your typical, puny wall calendar can get awfully hard to read. Nobody makes calendars with big enough date blanks for all your family's activities. Your home computer can change all that. Special calendar makers let you design your own daily, weekly, monthly, bi-weekly, semi-monthly—and, whatever-else-you-need calendars—all in minutes.

Now each family member can create calendars for every hobby or club in which they're involved. Young children will get a better grasp of organizing time once they sit down and enter in all their commitments. And you can hang specialized calendars where they'll do the most good—a gardening calendar inside a potting shed or garage, for example.

Calendar programs come with every sort of font and graphic with which to embellish your chronological creations, too. You can print appointments or regular meetings right on the calendar, or leave the dates blank and fill them in the low-tech way—with a pencil or marker.

COUPON AND REFUND SOFTWARE

Many people consider manufacturer's cents-off coupons too much of a bother, so they end up missing out on real savings—especially in stores that offer double coupon refunds. People who scoff at coupon redemption probably wouldn't mind getting a 66 percent raise when review time rolls around. Yet, if you double a dollar-off coupon and deduct that $2 from a $3 deodorant, you've just earned two-thirds more money.

Your home computer loves to organize you. Why not leave the tedium of sorting coupons to the computer? This type of software often comes with a database feature to track expiration dates, saving you possible embarrassment in the checkout line.

SOURCES FOR HOUSEHOLD APPLICATIONS SOFTWARE

Charting Home Energy Costs

- *Home Utility Recorder*, $5.00 (IBM/Compatibles, Macintosh)
  Heizer Software, 1941 Oak Park Blvd., Ste. 30
  Pleasant Hill, CA 94523, (415) 943-7667

- *Telisolar*, $50.00 (IBM/Compatibles)
  Tesseract Enterprises, LTD, 4334 140th St.
  Savage, MN 55378, (612) 894-9378

- *Homeowner*, $64.95 (IBM/Compatibles)
  Dynacomp, Inc., 178 Phillips Rd.
  Webster, NY 14580, (716) 265-4040

- *Wood Heat Calculator*, $19.99 (Apple Computers)
  Sourceview Software, Intl., P.O. Box 578
  Concord, CA 94522-0578, (415) 686-VIEW

Home Inventory/Household Records Software

- *Homeventory*, $24.95
  (Apple Computers, Commodore 64/128, IBM/Compatibles)
  Zephyr Services, 1900 Murray Ave.
  Pittsburgh, PA 15208, (412) 422-6600

- *Home Insurance Inventory*, $29.95 (IBM/Compatibles)
  Dynacomp, Inc., 178 Phillips Rd.
  Webster, NY 14580, (716) 265-4040

Holiday Applications

- *Christmas Sampler*, $15.00, *Christmas Story*, $12.00
  (IBM/Compatibles)
  Cross Educational Software, 504 E. Kentucky Ave.
  Ruston, LA 71270, (318) 255-8921

- *Christmas Concert* Vols 1 & 2 (Disks #1211, 1212), (IBM/Compatibles)
  PC-SIG, 1030 East Duane Avenue, Ste. D
  Sunnyvale, CA 94086, (800) 222-2996 (CA)
  (800) 245-6717 (USA), (408) 730-9291

- *Hyper Christmas Card*, $39.95 (Macintosh)
  Bright Ideas, Inc., 87A Ocean St.
  South Portland, ME 04106, (800) 272-1330

- *Hyperseder*, $34.95, *Vezot Hatorah*, $39.95
  High Holidays, $30.00 (many more, write for catalog), (Macintosh)
  Davka Corp., 845 N. Michigan Ave., Ste. 843
  Chicago, IL 60611, (800) 621-8227

Interior Decorator/Planning Software

- *Floorplan,* $49.00 (Apple Computers)
  Learning Seed Co., 6493 Kaiser Dr.
  Fremont, CA 94555, (415) 792-2101

- *Magic Mover*, $3.95/disk (IBM/Compatibles)
  Pan World International, P.O. Box 714
  Campbell, CA 95009

- *BDL.Move*, $39.95 (IBM/Compatibles)
  BDL Homeware, 2509 N. Campbell, #328M
  Tucson, AZ 85719

Label Makers/Calendar Programs

- *Labels Unlimited*, $64.95 (IBM/Compatibles)
  Power Up, Channelmark Corporation, 2929 Campus Dr.
  San Mateo, CA 94403, (800) 851-2917, (800) 223-1479 (in CA)

- *Create A Calendar*, $29.95
  (Apple Computers, Commodore 64/128, IBM/Compatibles)
  Epyx, P.O. Box 6041
  Sherman Oaks, CA 91413, (800) 826-4848, (415) 366-0606

- *Calendar Creator Plus*, $59.95 (IBM/Compatibles)
  Power Up, Channelmark Corporation, 2929 Campus Dr.
  San Mateo, CA 94403, (800) 851-2917, (800) 223-1479 (in CA)

Coupon and Refund Software

- *Coupon Organizer*, $39.95 (Apple Computers, IBM/Compatibles)
  Andent, Inc., 1000 North Ave.
  Waukegan, IL 60085, (312) 223-5077

- *Couponomizer*, $29.95 (IBM/Compatibles)
  Natural Software, Ltd., 19 S. Fifth St.
  St. Charles, IL 60174, (312) 377-7320

CHAPTER 2

Personal and Household Finance Software

People who use computers in their business wouldn't think of calculating expenses and income with a paper and pencil. Instead, they stick a spreadsheet on their computer and use the computer's power and speed to figure out whether they're making any money. Yet folks with a computer at home rarely take advantage of their computer's tireless ability to crunch numbers.

Of course, most businesses use big, memory-hungry, complex spreadsheets and databases to track profit and loss. Home computer users who just want to get a handle on their bank balance would never want or need all the features crammed into programs like Lotus *1-2-3*, Microsoft *Excel*, or *dBASE IV*. Yet most computer users would be surprised at the variety and convenience of personal and household finance software available.

Whether you balance a checkbook once a month, or play the stock market with nerves of steel, computer software can help you get, and stay, organized. Besides giving you the feeling that you're getting more use out of your home computer, personal finance software can save you time and maybe even money.

One note of caution: Make back-up diskettes frequently and regularly. These are your financial records we're talking about here. Computers are machines and as such are subject to mechanical failures—a fact to which I can attest only too painfully. So back up your records, preferably twice, and keep the second set in a different site altogether. End of sermon. We now return you to our regular programming.

TASKS FOR PERSONAL FINANCE SOFTWARE

- Track and Write Checks
- Assess Earnings and Financial Goals
- Organize and Pay Your Taxes
- Monitor Real Estate Holdings
- Evaluate Loans
- Watch Stock Market Investments
- Log Business Expenses

CHECKBOOK SOFTWARE

Keeping track of a checking account means more than throwing your statements and canceled checks into a "to-be-filed" folder and vaguely promising to get around to them sometime soon. Whether you've given up on ever balancing your checking account, or you'd just like to perform that monthly chore more quickly and easily, there's a checkbook balancing software program to fit your needs.

Although financial management software performs checkbook management too, you might not need or want to spend the time needed to learn all the bells and whistles of these bigger, more general programs. In this case, buy a dedicated checkbook-management program.

Features in checkbook management programs vary from tracking your check register to generating reports and spreadsheets. Several checkbook software programs even print out the check you've just logged by using special tractor-feed check forms you can special-order. You should look for checkbook management programs which can insert recurring payments. Make sure the program maintains more than one account at a time, as well.

Intuit's bestselling *Quicken* program for Apple, IBM/Compatible, and Macintosh computers can keep separate cash, credit card, and asset/liability accounts; preset home and business accounts with flags for tax items; print out longhand amounts in several check printing formats; perform automatic credit card reconciliation and payment; generate several reports, such as tracking tax-related items or travel expenses; and compare actual figures to a pre-programmed budget. *Andrew Tobias' Checkwrite Plus* forces you to be disciplined by assigning each payment to a category. This may seem tedious, but the records generated from such troublesome tasks are a godsend at tax time.

Imagine being able to pay bills electronically without ever having to mail a single envelope. Electronic checking systems such as *CheckFree* make it easy to stay organized—for a price. Besides paying bills, the program can handle routine banking, budgeting, and funds management—electronically, too. An automated check register can handle payment activity and record keeping. Reports are automatically generated, keeping you up to date on income, budget, and expenditures. Recurring bills like car payments are handled automatically, as well.

Although the convenience may be worthwhile if you live in a remote setting (lucky!), there's a one-time software/subscription cost of $49 plus a monthly fee of $10 (for up to 20 transactions). If you pay 20 bills a month, you can probably afford *CheckFree*. (Then again, maybe that means you *can't* afford *CheckFree*.) You'll need a modem and communications software, which, in tandem with *CheckFree*, lets you conduct your transactions directly with the Federal Reserve.

FINANCIAL MANAGEMENT SOFTWARE

Financial management software comes in many shapes and sizes. Generally, this category of computer program takes the basic function of checkbook management and expands it into every realm of personal and home finance. Now you can have an investment counselor, financial advisor, and bookkeeper for one low price—and the software package doesn't want to "do lunch" as often.

A financial management program should be able to not only track your checkbook and credit cards, but to determine how much insurance you should carry, to estimate your federal income taxes, and to set up your kid's college fund, as well. Databases handling these various financial areas are usually linked, supplying reports of one or all of the parts that make up your financial picture.

			Sales/AR				
			LEARNED LUMBER CO.	Debits	Credits		
			For the month of February, 1987				
Date	Description	Invoice#	Account#	Invoice Amount	Sales/Tax Amount	S T	T C
02/19	Cement Mix - 50 Bags/ A8899	23130	1050/0400	500.00			⬆
	50/ Bags Cement Mix		**Employees**				
02/25	190 6 by 8 - (5 Foot)		LEARNED LUMBER CO.				
	190/ 6 by 8 5 Foot Length		For the month of February, 1987				
02/26	Nails, Plywood and Doors	ID	Pay Type	Employee Name	Social Security #		
	50/ Boxes, #10 Nails						
	30/ Door Frames	1000	SALR	Brown, John J.	465-99-3567	⬆	
	400/ Sheets 3/4" Plywood	1050	SALR	Carson, John T.	111-22-3456		
		1100	HOUR	David, Sam R.	342-54-7738		

			Checking-CRJ					
			LEARNED LUMBER CO.		Total this Batch			
			For the month of February, 1987					
Date	Net Amt of Deposit	Received From/Description	Ref	Account#	Db	Amount	T C	
	' '	6.5% Sales Tax	Feb Wk 2	2015		117.00	⬆	
02/16	6163.16	Cash Sales	Feb Wk 3	4030/01		5592.00		
	' '	Cash Sales	Feb Wk 3	4030/02		195.00		
☞	' '	6.5% Sales Tax	Feb Wk 3	2015		376.16	⬇	
	02/23	260.93	Cash Sales	Feb Wk 4	4030/01		200.00	

Figure 3: Financial software keeps you out of the red.

A good financial program should help you set up a budget without too much trouble. Your investments should be easy to track. A good feature to look for is the ability to calculate your net worth. It's best to shop for the program that has features you think you'll use, because the high-end financial management programs can run into several hundred dollars.

After you've marveled at your net worth, it's a good idea to record all the whats, wheres, and whos in one place. You can keep essential information about your bank accounts, monthly bills, pensions, insurance policies, tax records, property holdings, and medical records handy with a program for IBM/Compatibles called *For the Record*.

This program features a question-and-answer session module that guides you (and prompts you to tell where the good silver is hidden). A manual comes with *For the Record* that discusses estate planning, taxes, legal records, and more. You can't take it with you, but *For the Record* lets you tell others where it is.

TAX SOFTWARE

Taxes. Sigh. No matter how prepared you think you are, there's always some essential information you can't locate at the last minute. Fortunately, many of the financial management programs already discussed in this chapter help you do tax planning earlier in the year before it's too late. For the actual tax return session, however, you'll want a tax preparation software package.

With the help of tax preparation software, your computer can help organize all the random bits of data into a meaningful 1040 form. Many tax programs work in conjunction with the financial management software programs and checkbook organizers mentioned above, so your data is already semi-organized. The beauty of tax programs is that, once entered, data is automatically entered on every significant line of the tax return.

One feature to look for is the simultaneous preparation of your state and federal returns. The better programs come with blank tax forms acceptable to the IRS, so your computer and printer work in tandem to produce a flawless, eraser-dust free tax return. Make sure the program you select offers automatic cross-checking of your input against data previously entered, to prevent mistakes. Several help screens are essential, as are IRS instruction screens that can be accessed when you need them.

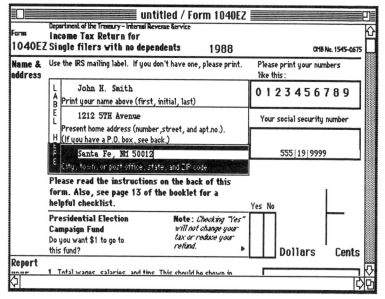

Figure 4: Income tax software forces you to get organized, while eliminating duplicate data entries.

REAL ESTATE SOFTWARE

In case you didn't already know, one of the fastest paths to riches (besides choosing wealthy parents) is buying and selling real estate. A good real estate software package can help you evaluate a property to make sure that fixer upper doesn't become a downer.

Most real estate management programs project rental income, in case you decide to become a land baron. Expenses, financing, cash flows, taxes, and resale values are all features you should look for in a real estate program. An obvious help would be the ability to figure adjustable and fixed-rate mortgages and depreciation.

RealData publishes a range of high-end real estate programs written for the Macintosh family of computers. Their *Property Management* I & II series can do everything for you if you own income property except keep those rent checks coming in on time.

(That part can't be enforced by any software program I know of!) The program features a detailed property profile, tenant statements, a cash receipts and cash disbursements journal, check printing, chart of accounts' financial statements, and much more.

LOAN SOFTWARE

Shopping for a loan can be a headache. Why not let your home computer do the numbers for you, instead? Many software programs out there can evaluate interest, fees, points, and more. A good loan evaluation software package will let you save various loan calculations to disk for comparison. You can use a spreadsheet to get the same results, but with these specialized programs, you just plug in the numbers. Programs are available for different types of loans, as well. How much will that new car *really* cost you?

Many people fail to realize how much money they could save on their mortgages if they were to pay a mere $25 extra per payment. Pre-payment is one of those secret financial tricks the guy in the BMW next to you at the stoplight knows. Now there's a software package to help you figure out how many thousands you can save with monthly prepayments. The package comes with a book explaining the finer points of the prepayment strategy. *Banker's Secret Software Package* for the IBM/Compatible family of computers will help you as a consumer.

STOCK MARKET SOFTWARE

Investing in the stock market can be risky, but the power of your home computer can help lessen that risk by keeping you organized. Portfolio management is easy with your computer's database capabilities, while your computer's spreadsheet can calculate the bottom line in a second. Many smaller programs are available to help you figure it all out.

High-end stock market programs are actually tied to on-line stock market databases that you access with your modem. These give you minute-by-minute updates. Hopefully, you're adept at the ins and outs of the market if you subscribe to the on-line databases, because fees run into hundreds of dollars per month. But even reasonably-priced programs like *Fundgraf* for IBM/Compatible computers produce stock market analyses and can graph and analyze funds or stocks.

EXPENSE LOGS

Although this book deals mainly with home uses for computers, the line between business and personal finances can sometimes blur. Do you ever travel for your company or home business? If the answer is "yes," you may welcome the convenience and efficiency of an expense log software program.

Programs like *Expense Master* for the IBM/Compatible family of computers can create reports for nonbillables, billable jobs, personal expenses, year-to-date expenses, credit cards, meals, entertainment, and other expenses. Reports can be custom-tailored to your fussy accounting department's standards.

Expense Master will let you enter your expenses in any order. This means that as you're pulling little bits of paper with numbers scrawled on them from your pockets and suitcase lining, you can run over to the computer and enter them into the software program. Voila! The program sorts the totals by category and date, and calculates everything. *Expense Master* offers a module that will convert foreign currencies, as well.

SOURCES FOR PERSONAL AND
HOUSEHOLD FINANCE SOFTWARE

Checkbook Software

- *Andrew Tobias' Checkwrite Plus*, $69.95 (IBM/Compatibles)
  MECA Ventures, Inc., 355 Riverside Ave.
  Westport, CT 06880, (800) 835-2246

- *Bank Mate*, $29.95 (IBM/Compatibles)
  Mindscape, Inc., 3444 Dundee Rd.
  Northbrook, IL 60062, (800) 221-9884

- *Checkbook Management* (Disk #393)
  PC-SIG, 1030 East Duane Avenue, Ste. D
  Sunnyvale, CA 94086, (800) 222-2996 (CA)
  (800) 245-6717 (USA), (408) 730-9291

- *CheckFree*, $49.95 (IBM/Compatibles)
  CheckFree Technologies, P/O. Box 897
  Colombus, OH 43216, (614) 898-6000

- *Check Tracker*, $19.95 (Commodore 64/128)
  Chipmunk Software, P.O. Box 463
  Battleground, WA 98604, (206) 687-2343

- *Check Writer*, $44.95 (IBM/Compatibles,Macintosh)
  Dynacomp, Inc., 178 Phillips Rd.
  Webster, NY 14580, (716) 265-4040

- *Checkkeeper*, $29.95 (IBM/Compatibles)
  Zephyr Services, 1900 Murray Ave.
  Pittsburgh, PA 15208, (412) 422-6600

- *Checkmaster-64*, $29.95 (Commodore 64/128)
  Dynacomp, Inc., 178 Phillips Rd.
  Webster, NY 14580, (716) 265-4040

- *How to Handle a Checking Account*, $49.00
  (Apple Computers, IBM/Compatibles)
  Learning Seed Co., 330 Telser Rd.
  Lake Zurich, IL 60047, (312) 540-8855

- *Money Mentor*, $99.95 (Amiga Computers)
  Sedona Software, 11828 Rancho Bernado Rd., Ste. 123
  San Diego, CA 92128, (619) 451-0151

- *Multiple Checkbook System*, $29.95 (Macintosh)
  Disk-Count Software, Inc., 1751 W. County Rd. B, Ste. 107
  Saint Paul, MN 55113, (612) 633-0730

- *Personal Accountant*, $49.95 (Macintosh)
  Softsync, Inc., 162 Madison Ave.
  New York, NY 10016, (212) 685-2080

- *Quicken*, $49.95 (Apple Computers, IBM/Compatibles, Macintosh)
  Intuit, 540 University Ave.
  Palo Alto, CA 94301, (415) 322-0573

- *Smart Checkbook*, $100.00 (Apple Computers, IBM/Compatibles)
  Softquest, Inc., P.O. Box 3456
  Mclean, VA 22103, (703) 281-1621

- *Smart Money*, $79.95 (Apple Computers, IBM/Compatibles)
  Sierra On-Line, Inc., P.O. Box 485
  Coarsegold, CA 93614, (209) 683-6858

Financial Management Software

- *Andrew Tobias' Managing Your Money*, $219.98
  (Macintosh, IBM/Compatibles)
  355 Riverside Ave., Westport, CT 06880
  (203) 222-9150, (800) 835-2246

- *Andrew Tobias' Financial Calculator*, $44.95 (IBM/Compatibles)
  355 Riverside Ave., Westport, CT 06880
  (203) 222-9150, (800) 835-2246

- *Business Sense*, $150.00 (Macintosh)
  Dollars and Sense, $149.95 (Macintosh)
  Monogram Software, 531 Van Ness Ave.
  Torrance, CA 90501, (213) 533-5120

- *For the Record*, $49.95 (IBM/Compatibles, Macintosh)
  Nolo Press, 950 Parker St.
  Berkeley, CA 94710, (415) 549-1976

- *MacMoney*, $119.95 (Macintosh)
  Survivor Software, 11222 La Cienega Blvd., #450
  Inglewood, CA 90304, (213) 410-9527

- *Money Counts*, $35.00 (IBM/Compatibles)
  Parsons Technology, 375 Collins Road NE
  Cedar Rapids, IO 52402, (800) 223-6925

- *Retirement Analyzer*, $25.00 (IBM/Compatibles, Macintosh)
  Heizer Software, 1941 Oak Park Blvd., Ste 30
  Pleasant Hill, CA 94523, (415) 943-7667

Tax Software

- *MacInTax*, $119.95 (Macintosh)
  TaxView, $119.95 (IBM/Compatibles)
  Softview, 4820 Adohr Lane, Ste. F
  Camarillo, CA 93010
- *TurboTax Personal*, $75.00 (IBM/Compatibles)
  ChipSoft, Inc., 5045 Shoreham Dr.
  San Diego, CA 92122, (619) 453-8722

Real Estate Software

- *Landlord* (Disk #585), (IBM/Compatibles)
  California Freeware, 1747 E. Ave. Z, Unit C-1
  Palmdale, CA 93550, (805) 273-0300
- *PropMan* ((Disk #1179, 1180, 1452), (IBM/Compatibles)
  PC-SIG, 1030 East Duane Avenue, Ste. D
  Sunnyvale, CA 94086, (800) 222-2996 (CA)
  (800) 245-6717 (USA), (408) 730-9291
- *Real Estate Investment Analysis*, $195.00
  Property Managemen, $295.00 (Macintosh)
  Real Data, 78 North Main St.
  South Norwalk, CT 06854, (203) 255-2732
- *Real Estate Analyst* (Disk #083), (IBM/Compatibles)
  California Freeware, 1747 E. Ave. Z, Unit C-1
  Palmdale, CA 93550, (805) 273-0300

Loan Software

- *Auto Finance Analyzer*, $9.00 (IBM/Compatibles, Macintosh)
  Heizer Software, 1941 Oak Park Blvd., Ste 30
  Pleasant Hill, CA 94523, (415) 943-7667
- *Loan Analysis*, $21.95 (IBM/Compatibles)
  Dynacomp, Inc.

- *Loan Manager*, $49.95 (IBM/Compatibles)
  Lassen Software, Inc., P.O. Box 2319
  Paradise, CA 95967-2319, (916) 877-0408

- *Loan Payoff Analysis*, $6.00 (Macintosh)
  Heizer Software, 1941 Oak Park Blvd., Ste 30
  Pleasant Hill, CA 94523, (415) 943-7667

- *Banker's Secret Software Package*, $29.95 (IBM/Compatibles)
  Good Advice Press, P.O. Box 78
  Elizaville, NY 12523, (800) 255-0899

Stock Market Software

- *Fundgraf*, $100.00 (IBM/Compatibles)
  Parsons Software, 1230 W. 6th St., Dept. C
  Loveland, CO 80537, (303) 669-3744

- *PC-Stock* (Disk #575), (IBM/Compatibles)
  PC-SIG, 1030 East Duane Avenue, Ste. D
  Sunnyvale, CA 94086, (800) 222-2996 (CA)
  (800) 245-6717 (USA), (408) 730-9291

- *StockFolio*, $39.95 (IBM/Compatibles)
  Zephyr Services, 1900 Murray Ave.
  Pittsburgh, PA 15208, (412) 422-6600

- *Wall Street Investor*, $695.00 (Macintosh, IBM/Compatibles)
  Pro Plus Software, Inc., 2150 E. Brown rd.
  Mesa, AZ 85203, (800) 227-5728

Business Expense Software

- *Expense Account Manager*, $99.00
   (Apple Computers, IBM/Compatibles)
  Adaptive Software, 1866 Sheridan Rd., Ste. 301
  Highland Park, IL 60035

- *Expense Master*, $69.95 (IBM/Compatibles)
  Danart Corp, 76 Belvedere St.
  San Rafael, CA 94901, (415) 461-9100

PART TWO

CHAPTER 3

Computerize Your Hobbies and Collections

Hobbies are all those things we do for fun besides work. (For some lucky folks, the line between work and play sometimes blurs a little.)

People come up with the most unusual ways to spend their spare time. There was a guy who collected horse's kidney stones, for example (all right, so he *was* a vet!); a woman who assembled paintings from dryer lint; and a man who ate an entire train, locomotive first.

For most of us, however, hobbies fall into more mundane categories: collections—or creative, technical, or social pursuits.

Your home computer can increase the fun of hobbies like stamp collecting, restoring old cars, or creative writing by keeping you organized.

TASKS FOR HOBBY SOFTWARE

- Log Ham Radio Contacts
- Design Sewing, Needlepoint, and Weaving Projects
- Catalogue Coin, Stamp, and Other Collections
- Organize Photos, Slides, and Albums
- Compose and Edit Music
- Enhance Creative Writing Skills

- Catalogue Family Ties
- Create Club Newsletters/Track Club Memberships

HAM RADIO SOFTWARE

Before there were computer nerds (before there were home computers!) there were Ham Radio enthusiasts. With terminology like "input impedances," "reactive frequency values," and "coil inductance," this hobby makes modeming look like hopscotch. Now the old and the new can merge when you use your home computer to organize your ham radio activities.

A number of shareware diskettes provide the ham radio enthusiast with many fun and useful programs. It seems that many ham radio users write shareware programs when they're not cruising the airwaves.

Ham Radio #1 offers three different Morse code programs to help the user learn and review data. Other routines help the amateur radio operator compute various electronic formulas, design antennas, find satellites, and calculate satellite orbits. Two communications programs are included, and a program is featured that takes audio (speaker output) and converts tones to a picture format. The user with a shortwave receiver can receive, view, and print pictures from the ham operators. You need to have a version of BASIC loaded onto your computer to run this program.

Ham Radio #2 features a program for real-time tracking of the OSCAR 9 and five other satellites, programs that calculate coil inductance, coil properties, signals for varying frequencies, resistance and reactance, and more. An alphabetized list of all the counties in each state can be found in this information-packed program, as well. These IBM/Compatible programs require BASIC and 128K RAM; the RDSSTV2 file requires a color graphics display.

Many ham radio enthusiasts enter contests to see how many other enthusiasts they can contact. Whoever calls the most people is eligible for awards. An amateur radio contest-logging program called *KB0ZP Super Contest Log* helps the operator log all those contacts. You can print out the log in a suitable format and enter them for prizes.

KB0ZP Super Contest Log's main screen shows date and time, name of contest, station call sign, grand total number of contacts made by mode and band, elapsed time from last contact, and total accumulated score. Up to 4,000 contacts can be logged. The program even includes help screens showing usable frequencies by band, class of license, and section abbreviations. For those amateur radio operators on the go, the program features a "hurry-up timer" that can time each contact.

Other software of interest to the ham radio enthusiast includes *MiniMuf*, a MUF (Maximum Usable Frequency) calculator for the amateur radio operator; *Morse*, a Morse Code-learning program; *Bearings*, for radio amateurs or anyone needing the precise bearings or great circle directions from one location to another; and *PC-Ham*, a set of amateur radio database programs (BASIC and *dBASE II* are required for *PC-Ham*).

SEWING, WEAVING, AND NEEDLECRAFT SOFTWARE

The home computer's graphics capabilities are ideally suited to garment design. Whether your medium is cloth, yarn, or embroidery floss, sewing and crafts software can help you map out your project in advance—before time-consuming mistakes occur.

Weaving Software

Weaving is basically the creation of a grid, using yarns and other materials instead of paper and pen. Weaving software runs the gamut, from simple grid creation and viewing in a program like Compucrafts' *Weaver*, to a high-end, professional-quality software program like *Design & Weave*, which provides tools and options to let you produce exquisite and complex fabrics.

Design & Weave's features include viewing and revising finished patterns on screen; printing a copy of a pattern plus all the technical information necessary to weave it; automatically computing plain weaves, twills and satins; combining two designs into one for more complex structures; performing repeats, symmetries, and picking motions, and more.

You can combine this program with other tools. With a plotter you can print out colored designs. Hooked up to a color monitor, you can see 16.7 million colors. The program zooms in and out to four different thread sizes; creates drawdowns and patterns for any loom; interfaces with the AVL Compu-Dobby system, and more.

Sewing Software

SewSoft Bodice for the Macintosh is designed to bring speed and simplicity to the creation of custom-fitted shirts and blouses. It's easy to keep measurements in the database with a home computer next to your sewing machine.

To tailor clothing ten personal body measurements can be altered. These measurements specify a basic bodice, sloper or master pattern, which is printed onto six or more pages of standard printer paper. These pages are joined to form a full-size, precise pattern from which garments can be cut and sewn.

The program can be modified to produce a new sloper whenever there is a significant weight loss or gain. So, there's no need to cut down on those creme eclairs—your clothes will always fit.

SewSoft Bodice accommodates any adult body size or shape for blouses, tops, or shirts. It also facilitates the adjustment of commercial patterns to individual shapes, and can be used to modify styles and copy the design of a ready-made garment.

An illustrated users' manual explains the measurement-taking system, and a variety of screen displays guide a user through the operation of the system. Extra measurement forms are also provided.

For the Apple computer family, a program called *Patchworks* can help you come up with alternatives to the same old patchwork patterns. The program quickly generates a wide range of geometric shapes, which you can shape and edit on-screen. Print out the pieces when you're satisfied with the design. You can then lay them out on cardboard, to create templates, and you're ready to create an original, high-tech quilt or wall hanging.

Needlecraft Software

Drawing up designs for needlepoint or embroidery can be messy and time-consuming. A program called *Stitch Grapher* for the Apple family of computers lets you draw, edit, save, and print needlecraft creations. If you don't have an Apple computer, you can use one of the many drawing programs to achieve the same goal.

If you knit you know that charting curves and other tricky parts of your garment could be easier. *Mom's Knitting Computer Program* for the Apple can help. Templates for necklines, sleeves, collars, and more can be filled in, edited, and printed out. Now you can knit something more complex than scarves and socks for Christmas gifts.

COIN AND STAMP COLLECTION SOFTWARE

Computers are perfect devices for keeping track of collections. The power of databases to search, sort, and print data retrievals makes it a breeze to confirm the issue date of your obscure Guianan stamp. Spreadsheet features like automatic price updates let you keep an eye on the current market value of those priceless Spanish coins.

Collections aren't limited to stamps and coins, though. I went to a convention and met a guy who specializes in collecting vintage *TV Guide* magazines. The moral is, don't throw anything away, ever. And let your computer help keep it organized.

Specialized software tailored to stamp and coin collectors combines spreadsheet and database features and even offers simple text editors for word processor functions. If you don't collect stamps or coins, there are catch-all collection organizers available. If you don't find any software you can use, customize a simple database or spreadsheet program to your needs. In any case, collections are more enjoyable when you can see at a glance just what you've collected!

COINS/PLUS is a coin inventory program that contains the descriptions and latest market value price information on more than 2,300 U.S. coins.

The program uses convenient standard coin numbers and shows current market values. It provides written records for investment, tax, insurance, and estate planning purposes and tracks the value of your investment, automatically updating prices each year.

Comprehensive reports include: Value Report, which lists coins in a user's collection, what you paid for each coin, current value and resulting profit or loss to date; Collection Summary report, which provides bottom line figures such as total number of coins in a collection, total amount paid for them and total present value; Coins Sold Report, detailing cost and profit figures on coins you've sold; and Want List, a buyer's guide in which you can indicate the coins needed to complete your collection.

The IBM/Compatibles shareware program *Coin File* keeps an inventory of coins and a want list and will print out an inventory sheet as well as mini labels for your coins.

The publisher of *COINS/PLUS* put out two sister programs that operate similarly to that program but are designed for stamp collectors. *STAMPS WORLD* helps inventory and evaluate your international or topical stamp collection. *STAMPS* keeps track of all your U.S. stamps. Both programs generate the extensive reports of *COINS/PLUS*, as well.

Commodore and IBM/Compatible computer owners can get organized with *Collector's Paradise*, which contains inventory programs for coin collections, stamp collections, and rare collectibles. Another catch all collection organizer is *The Collector*.

PHOTOGRAPHY SOFTWARE

Most of you have all your photos neatly tucked into well-captioned photo albums, lined up in tidy rows on your bookshelves, right? Well, if you throw those carefully composed photos in the nearest shoebox the minute you get home from that vacation or family reunion (like everyone else), you can benefit from photography software. Organize those pictures (with the help of your computer) so they can be seen and enjoyed.

Most photo software offers the same basic features. There's usually a database and a labeling feature, keeping your voice from going hoarse after explaining all 12 rolls of vacation film. Your friends can simply read the label on the back of the picture, instead. To choose photo software, determine what type of program will best suit your needs. Some programs are designed for commercial photographers, while others are better suited to home uses.

Pic Trak is a photo, slide, and album cataloguing system designed for people who want to organize business and personal photos for showing. This program is easy to get up and running and comes with free telephone support (although a long-distance call to Montana is required). The assortment of labels included runs from slide captions to labels for the backs of your photos.

STOCKvue is designed for the professional photographer. This program generates captions, catalogue entries, and submissions logs. The photographer who has trouble keeping track of when, where, and to whom photos were sent will appreciate this last feature. It dates submissions to tell you when photos are due back, noting when they are late. A menu selection even prints a customized form letter to remind a client of how many photographs are late and who received them. Data for each photograph tells you the photo's creator, film type, format, model releases, value, and earned income.

Two shareware programs for IBM/Compatible computers fill the needs of camera bugs for less money. *For Photographers* spans the needs of hobbyists and professionals alike. This program lets you decide how detailed your photo records will be. The Basic level is for minimal record keeping. The Photographer level goes into processing, printing, and other data about a particular photo. The third level, Professional, adds client information. *Photo Pack* is a collection of programs to help improve photo skills. There's a lens selection module, a darkroom timer program, a label maker, and a photo database.

MUSIC SOFTWARE

Composing and editing music on your computer is just as easy as composing and editing words on your computer. Hundreds of music software programs make exploring the world of sharps and trebles fun—and guarantee a measure of privacy for those who should be playing the radio, instead!

One of the most powerful composing tools available for both amateur and professional musicians, and those who just want to fool around, is *Deluxe Music Construction Set*. This program is available for the Macintosh and Commodore Amiga brands of computers—both of which excel in making music.

Deluxe Music Construction Set turns your computer into a desktop-based professional music publishing studio. Complete input, editing, and notation tools help with quick compositions. Music is entered, edited, and reviewed in a Score Window. Music may be entered into the program from the built-in library, or notes may be arranged on the staff by selecting them from the Note Palette or by playing them with the mouse via the program's piano keyboard. Lots of cut and paste options make editing a breeze.

One of *Deluxe Music Construction Set*'s more advanced features is a voice editor, which lets you create and modify your own warblings and add them to your compositions. Fun stuff! Once you've got it down, you can see what's going on in three ways: a measure counter, flashing notes, and a player piano. Other advanced features included creating staccato, smooth, and vibrato sound effects; the ability to change parameters like key and time signatures, staffs and clefs, working space and score width; and the option of repeating scores and passages without actually replaying the piece.

Desktop music publishers take note: *Deluxe Music Construction Set* supports Adobe's Sonata font. Typeset quality musical scores can be yours with the use of a laser printer.

Anybody with a serious interest in music should try out this program. There's even an IBM/Compatible and an Apple version (with less features) called *Music Construction Set*.

On the shareware front, several programs for IBM/Compatible computers let you try before you buy. *Composer* lets you easily create and edit music. *PC-Musician* is geared for the beginner,

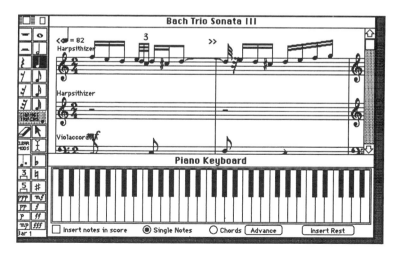

Figure 5: It's fun and easy to create and play music with a number of music programs.

teaching notation as you enter music and play it back. *Piano* turns your PC into a piano. Unfortunately, the PC only plays one note at a time, so you can't play chords, but you can change the pitch and duration of your notes. *Pianoman* is a bit more advanced, allowing cut and paste, and even search and replace!

Those involved in choirs and other music groups should check out *The Music Minder*. This music library management system can keep track of music orders, music library inventory, and performances. Some of the features include a music library filing system, complete music ordering information, individual 3- by 5-inch music library card printing, performance tracking, establishment of multiple libraries, performance history reports, and other reports based on composer, key words, and titles. CGA color capability is required.

CREATIVE WRITING SOFTWARE

Picture yourself, feather-quill pen in hand, composing beautiful verse and exciting fiction. Now picture yourself, keyboard in hand, learning how to craft all that verse and fiction. The computer can tutor you in writing well, whether your writing hobby centers around fiction or poetry.

Writer's Workshop for the Macintosh offers writers and researchers the ability to organize freelance writing ideas, finances, and reference materials.

Three modules track financial records (for when you become good enough to get paid for your writing), ideas and submissions, and references. Searches and reports can be easily generated.

WritePro for IBM/Compatibles teaches creative writing. Proven fiction writing techniques culled from the collected experience of hundreds of professional writers come in the form of interactive lessons. The program can banish the dreaded Writer's Block for good.

Three programs for the IBM/Compatible family of computers help you capture the poetic muse. *Poetry Processor* is a word processor designed for writing poetry or lyrics. Pre-set poetic forms make creating a sonnet a matter of simply plugging in lines. A model for that style can appear in a window at the top of your screen to help you get it right. After completing your poem, the rhyme scheme is checked. The program checks for the correct number of lines, feet, beats, syllables, etc. You can check a work of up to 99 lines. If your poem is longer, simply split it into two or more parts. You can save the results in the program's internal anthology.

By the same publisher, *Orpheus* is a collection of all the poetic forms, over 20 of them. The program explains the origin and purpose behind each form. Now you'll be able to dash off a terzanelle in no time. The third program in the trilogy is *Newman's Electronic Rhyming Dictionary (N.E.R.D.). N.E.R.D.* is a utility that can find rhymes for any word.

In addition, hundreds of style and grammar checkers are available for every computer system. Mentioned before in the educational software section, *Readability* for IBM/Compatible computers is one of the best writing aids around. Save an example of your writing as a text file, and bring it into *Readability.* Choose one of nine categories of writing you think it fits.

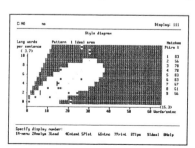

Figure 6: Readability *shows you what type of writing you do best.*

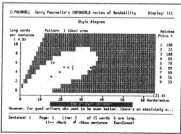

Figure 7: Readability *flags awkward sentences and shows how you can improve them.*

Categories range from "Children's books" to "Magazine feature articles" to "Bureaucratic gobbledygook." (I wonder if anybody ever chooses this last category.) You can see at a glance how your writing measures up in any of 16 diagrams. Suggestions for increasing your writing's readability follow. The hardcover manual is extensive and well researched.

MacProof for the Macintosh is a text review software program that helps writers become more aware of the choices they make in writing. Writing is viewed more as a process in this program. The mechanics module includes review programs for checking spelling, punctuation, capitalization and double words. The usage module checks words that might be offensive, sexist, or racist. It sets off words that are commonly confused, terms that are imprecise, expressions that are trite, and words generally regarded as slang. *MacProof* has style and structure modules as well.

GENEALOGY SOFTWARE

Genealogy is a popular hobby, judging by the number and scope of available genealogy software. Computer database and report generating capabilities are natural helpmates to the detailed records necessary for genealogists. Computer graphics capabilities let you make neat coats of arms and other genealogy-oriented art and awards.

The two top-selling genealogy programs for the PC are *Roots III* and *Personal Ancestral File*. Both programs let you create reports and charts based on names, locations, and years. You can even publish formal family histories. *Roots III* can chart up to six generations per page, and the program automatically numbers and references continuation pages. Ancestor charts and family-group sheets let you easily calculate blood relationships between any two subjects. The manual weighs in at over 750 pages, answering all the genealogy questions you could ever dream up.

On the Macintosh front, *MacGene* lets you annotate individual records with baptism, occupation, military service details, and more. You can link records for fast access to charts, lists, and sorts. *Family Heritage File* can produce approved submission forms for all Latter-day Saints ordinances, as well as lists of individuals whose ordinance work has not yet been completed. *Family Roots* allows direct insertion of word processor files, letting you tell all the family secrets in as much detail as you want.

Shareware programs for IBM/Compatibles let you try out the hobby and see if it's for you. *Family Ties* and *Family History* offer all the database capabilities the beginner is likely to need.

The *Heraldry* program for the Macintosh makes designing your own (or others') coats of arms fun and educational too. If you're not a blueblood, all the better—see how wild a coats of arms you can think up. These make thoughtful, personalized gifts for members of genealogy groups and non-members alike.

CLUB/HOBBY GROUP SOFTWARE

Even though desktop publishing is really more "productivity" software, and thus beyond the scope of this book, it's nice to be able to generate newsletters and such when your hobby involves you as a member in a club or other social group. One easy and fun program for simple desktop publishing should be mentioned in this section.

The IBM/Compatible *Pages* desktop publishing program is a welcome addition to the software collections of active club and social group members. You can generate professional-looking newsletters, forms, assignments, handouts, reports, or articles, and thrill fellow club members with your speed and efficiency in getting the word out.

Pages fills the gap between complex, high-end desktop publishing programs that take too much memory to run and too much time to learn, and low priced, entry-level programs that are little more than glorified word processors. Quality page layout is finally accessible with this sophisticated, yet reasonably-priced and easy-to-learn program.

Pouring your word processor documents into *Pages* is facilitated by the icon/graphic menu interface. Although you can create text right in *Pages*, you'll prefer the power and familiarity your word processor gives.

Once you've created and saved the text, you can choose one of *Pages*' seven "style sheets," or pre-formatted page formats: two-column text, three-column with headline, and so on. *Pages* emulates the most sophisticated desktop publishing programs by offering several templates, pre-designed, or custom document layouts (more complex than style sheets).

Once inside your chosen style sheet or template, you select a box for the imported text to be poured into. Longer word processor files may require the linking of several boxes. You merely click on the Open Text tool in the Master Toolbox or select Open from the File menu. Indicate the directory and path where your word processor file is from the dialog box's file display and double-click on your word processor filename.

The text pours automatically into your *Pages* document, wrapping around pictures or boxes and into the next column. Columnar text can be justified, centered, flush right or flush left. *Pages* includes a search and replace feature that can save endless hours of typing while completing that final editing on screen.

Once you've poured in your text, you'll want to fine-tune the document with carefully selected font (type style) and graphics options. Remember, less is more when mixing typography and design elements like borders, type sizes, hairlines, italics, and graphics.

Even though *Pages* offers a wide range of such tools, you don't want to use them all at once!

In case you do get a little carried away, the Undo option, another savvy *Pages* feature common to "high-end" desktop publishing programs, can save the day. Undo reverses your last action. When you select Undo from the menu, your document automatically reverts to the way it was before you gave the unwanted command—or a dialog box informs you that the action can't be undone.

They say a picture is worth a thousand words, and just about any document can benefit from an illustration or two. *Pages* can open picture files from the following programs: *The Print Shop*, *GEM Paint*, *PC Paintbrush*, *First Publisher*, *MacPaint* (yes, you heard right!), and several others. With all the great public domain clip art available for the Macintosh, *Pages'* ability to import and utilize Macintosh graphics files renders it outstanding for educational purposes.

The process of importing picture files is identical to that of importing word processor files, except that the picture appears right in the middle of the document window. It can then be sized and moved wherever you want. If the picture isn't quite what you need, you can use *Pages'* Magnify tool to touch up, smooth, or even embellish imported pictures. The Crop tool is invaluable for balancing a picture's visual elements. What's more, *Pages* offers advanced object-oriented graphics capabilities, superior to paint-program output for designing your own art. Once created, you can rotate, flip, reverse, or duplicate objects at will.

Printing your document is the final step, and *Pages* shows a great deal of consideration in allowing you to set up your printer to low, medium, or high resolution before printing. The "low" setting is handy for when you just want to print a quick draft.

On Track

Keeping track of club and group members can turn a hobby into a full-time job! A shareware program for IBM/Compatible computers can serve as a membership database for any group or club, as well as for churches. *Church Membership System* tracks members' birthdays and anniversaries, as well as other important dates. Special features include modify/delete, browsing, and multiple reports.

A program called *Who, What, When* helps manage group members, projects, and more. This is another program taken from the "productivity" software category, but it's ideally suited to keeping track of a busy club or social group. Meetings, people, and projects can be logged, and reports generated. A binder allows you to have a "hardcopy" of plans on hand anytime.

Prized Members

Awards and prizes are natural parts of club and hobby group doings. *Award Maker Plus* and *Certificate Maker* let you print professional quality awards, certificates, licenses, coupons, or similar documents. Both programs include hundreds of pre-designed templates. Menu selection makes using these programs easy and fun.

HOBBY SOFTWARE

Ham Radio Software

- *Ham Radio #1* (Disk #436, 437), *Ham Radio #2* (Disk #1420)
  KB0ZP Super Contest Log (Disk #1096), *MiniMuf* (Disk #1315)
  Morse (Disk #939), *PC-Ham* (Disk #562)
  (IBM/Compatibles)
  PC-SIG, 1030 East Duane Avenue, Ste. D
  Sunnyvale, CA 94086, (800) 222-2996 (CA)
  (800) 245-6717 (USA), (408) 730-9291

- *Bearings* , $19.95 (Apple)
  Zephyr Services, 1900 Murray Ave.
  Pittsburgh, PA 15217

Weaving Software

- *Design & Weave*, $300.00 (Macintosh)
  AVL Looms, 601 Orange St.
  Chico, CA 95928, (916) 893-4915, (800) 626-9615

- *Weaver*, $49.95 (Apple Series)
  Compucrafts, P.O. Box 326
  Lincoln Center, MA 01773, (508) 263-8007

Sewing Software

- *SewSoft Bodice* , $59.95 (Macintosh)
  Andros SoftWear, P.O. Box 782
  Moss Beach, CA 94038, (415) 728-3553

- *Patchworks*, $49.95 (Apple Computers)
  McGraw Hill Media, 11 W. 19th St.
  NY, NY 10022, (212) 572-2433

Needle Crafts Software

- *Stitch Grapher*, $89.95 (Apple Computers, IBM/Compatibles)
  Compucrafts, P.O. Box 326
  Lincoln Center, MA 01773, (508) 263-8007

Knitting Software

- *Mom's Knitting Computer Program*, $49.99
  (Apple Computers and IBM/Compatibles)
  Triple-D Software, 823 N. 1340 E.
  Layton, UT 84041, (801) 547-9328

Collection Tracking Software

- *COINS/PLUS* , $95.00
  (IBM/Compatibles, Macintosh and Apple Computers)
  Compu-Quote, 6914 Berquist Ave.
  Canoga Park, CA 91307, (818) 348-3662, (800) 782-6775

- *Coin File*, (IBM/Compatibles)
  Pan World International, 422 Halsey Rd.
  N. Brunswick, NJ 08902, (201) 821-6164
  831 Dale Dr., #67, Campbell, CA 95008

- *Stamps World*, $65.00
  (Apple Computers, IBM/Compatibles, Macintosh)
  Compu-Quote, 6914 Berquist Ave.
  Canoga Park, CA 91307, (818) 348-3662, (800) 782-6775

- *Collector's Paradise*
  (IBM/Compatibles) $39.95, (Commodore 64/128) $29.95
  Coindata, $49.95 (IBM/Compatibles)
  Dynacomp, Inc., 178 Phillips Rd.
  Webster, NY 14580, (716) 265-4040

- *Stamp Collector*, $49.00 (Apple Computers, IBM/Compatibles)
  Coin Collector Catalog, $49.00 (Apple Computers, IBM/Compatibles)
  Andent, Inc., 1000 North Ave.
  Waukegan, IL 60085, (312) 223-5077

- *The Collector*, $85.00 (IBM/Compatibles)
  The Third Rail, 3377 Cimmaron Dr.
  Santa Ynez, CA 93460, (805) 688-7370

Photography Software

- *Pic Trak*, $89.00 (IBM/Compatibles)
  P.O. Box 3358, Missoula, MT 59806
  (406) 251-5870, (800) 234-5026

- *STOCKvue*, $99.95 (Macintosh)
  HindSight, P.O. Box 11608
  Denver, CO 80211, (303) 458-6372

- *For Photographers* (Disk #1164)
  Photo Pack (Disk #1249)
  (IBM/Compatibles)
  PC-SIG, 1030 East Duane Avenue, Ste. D
  Sunnyvale, CA 94086, (800) 222-2996 (CA)
  (800) 245-6717 (USA), (408) 730-9291

Music Software

- *Deluxe Music Construction Set*, $99.95 (Macintosh, Commodore Amiga)
  Music Construction Set, $14.95 (Apple Computers, IBM/Compatibles)
  Electronic Arts, 1820 Gateway Dr.
  San Mateo, CA 94404, (415) 571-7171

- *Composer* (Disk #794), *The Music Minder* (Disk #1472)
  PC-Musician (Disk #127), *Piano* (Disk #322), *Pianoman* (Disk #279)
  (IBM/Compatibles)
  PC-SIG, 1030 East Duane Avenue, Ste. D
  Sunnyvale, CA 94086, (800) 222-2996 (CA)
  (800) 245-6717 (USA), (408) 730-9291

Creative Writing Software

- *Writer's Workshop*, $99.00
  Futuresoft System Designs, Inc., 160 Bleecker St., #5JW
  NY, NY 10012, (212) 674-5195

- *Poetry Processor*, $89.95, *Orpheus*, $49.95
  Newman's Electronic Rhyming Dictionary, $59.95 (IBM/Compatibles)
  Michael Newman, c/o The Paris Review, 541 E. 72nd St.
  NY, NY 10021, (201) 525-2122

- *Readability*, $94.95 (IBM/Compatibles)
  Scandinavian PC Systems, Inc., 51 Monroe St., Ste. 707A
  Rockville, MA 20850, (301) 738-8826

- *MacProof* , $195.00 (Macintosh)
  Automated Language Processing systems, 295 Chipeta Way
  Salt Lake City, UT 84108, (801) 584-3000, (800) 354-5656

Genealogy Software

- *Roots III* , $250.00 (IBM/Compatibles)
  Commsoft, 2257 Old Middlefield Way
  Mountain View, CA 94043, (415) 967-1900

- *Personal Ancestral File*, $35.00 (IBM/Compatibles)
  Church of Jesus Christ of Latter-day Saints, 50 E. North Temple St.
  Salt Lake City, UT 84150, (801) 531-2584

- *MacGene*, $145.00 (Macintosh)
  Applied Ideas, Inc., P.O. Box 3225
  Manhattan Beach, CA 90266, (213) 545-2996

- *Family Heritage*, $149.00 (Macintosh)
  Starcom Software Systems, 25 West 1480 North
  Orem, UT 84057, (801) 225-1480

- *Family Roots*, $72.50 (Macintosh)
  Quinsept, Inc., P.O. Box 216
  Lexington, MA 02173, (617) 641-2930

- *Family Ties* (Disk #465)
  Family History (Disks #361, #632)
  (IBM/Compatibles)
  PC-SIG, 1030 East Duane Avenue, Ste. D
  Sunnyvale, CA 94086, (800) 222-2996 (CA)
  (800) 245-6717 (USA), (408) 730-9291

- *Family Tree* , $49.95 (Commodore Amiga)
  Micromaster Software, 1289 Brodhead Rd.
  Monaca PA 15061, (412) 775-3000

- *Heraldry*, $39.95 (Macintosh)
  Pleasant Graphic Ware, P.O. Box 506
  Pleasant Hill, OR 97455, (503) 345-5796

Club/Social Group Software

- *Pages*, $79.95
  Pinpoint Publishing, 5865 Doyle, Ste. 112
  Emeryville, CA 94608, (707) 935-3050

- *Church Membership System* (Disk #742)
  PC-SIG, 1030 East Duane Avenue, Ste. D
  Sunnyvale, CA 94086, (800) 222-2996 (CA)
  (800) 245-6717 (USA), (408) 730-9291

- *Who, What, When* , $189.95 (IBM/Compatibles)
  Chronos Software, Inc., 1500 16th St., Ste. 100
  San Francisco, CA 94103, (800) 777-7907

- *Award Maker Plus*, $49.95 (Macintosh)
  Baudville, 5380 52nd St. SE
  Grand Rapids, MI 49508, (616) 957-3036

- *Certificate Maker*, $34.95 (Macintosh)
  Springboard Software, Inc., 7808 Creekridge Cir.
  Minneapolis, MN 55435, (612) 944-3915

Chapter 4

Let (Your Computer)
Entertain You

Computers weren't designed for games originally. You can guess this just by looking at their small, monochrome monitors and by hearing their tinny little speakers. But equipped with today's color monitors, sound enhancers, and game software, computers provide one of the best possible sources of entertainment around the house. Now, not every game is going to appeal to you. But loaded with the right game software, you and your computer can get lost for hours. Where else can you find so much entertainment without aggravating anybody or spending lots of money?

Games fall into a few basic categories. After reading about one or two games from each category, you'll get an idea of whether that type of game appeals to you. Don't be afraid to explore! Thousands of computer games out there are just waiting for your mouse, joystick, or arrow keys. There are even magazines devoted solely to computer gaming.

If you like a quest and don't mind typing, the text-adventure brand of computer game is for you. These games transport you to lost worlds, the distant past, or even the golden city of Lost Wages. The text-adventure game was the first widely popular category of computer game (not counting Pong).

The first text-adventure games had patchy xxxs and lines for graphics, but that was back in the computer Dark Ages. (Examples of these early text-adventure games are still available on BBSs for comparison's sake—rough stuff, but you can still spend hours playing with them.) Today's text adventure games are an art form unto themselves—particularly the sound-and-animation extravaganzas put out by companies like Sierra On-line and Accolade.

Perhaps you've always wanted to lead a tank platoon into bloody combat. Well, me neither, but *somebody's* buying the many realistic computer simulation games out there. Each new computer simulation title that comes out represents years of research-and-development-hours getting the details right. With simulation software loaded into your computer, everything from battles at sea to open-heart surgery can be enacted right in your computer room.

If you're tired of dumping quarters into arcade video games, you can load your home computer with arcade-quality games to rival even the meanest, most screaming video game. Save those quarters to buy the inevitable joystick, though. And with sports software, you can become the brains behind the brawn. Every team has its leader, and your computer can put you in charge.

CATEGORIES OF COMPUTER GAMES

- Adventure Games
- Simulation Software
- Arcade Games
- Sports Software

Adventure Games

First off, a couple of clues about the text-adventure game category. (You're certainly not going to get any help from the game or manual itself!) The first time you play an adventure game, the learning curve can be a little steep. You're just not used to typing in, "Look at floor" or "Look at ceiling" every time you see a new screen. But unless you interact with the game by typing as many commands as possible (and some impossible ones, too), the text-adventure game can go as dead as the freeways on New Year's morning.

A second hint for playing adventure games: Save the game to disk anytime you pass some kind of hurdle and get points for it. Adventure games are played by going around the game's little world with your little character, collecting as many objects as you can find and saying whatever off-the-wall things occur to you to everyone you meet. Objects you gather are going to be crucially essential to completing the quest at some further point in the game. If you don't save the game frequently, though, and then you get in trouble, you'll lose everything.

A third hint for playing adventure games: try every possible move you can think of before sending away for the hint book. These books are readily available from the game's publishers, but the whole hint book concept is kind of a ripoff.

If you like sarcasm, poor taste, and racy, X-rated graphics, try the *Leisure Suit Larry* series of text-adventure games from Sierra On-line. In *Leisure Suit Larry in the Land of the Lounge Lizards*, Larry found himself in the City of Lost Wages, looking for, well, what Larry is always looking for: someone curvy, preferably a blond, brunet, redhead, or bald! In other words, Larry will take anyone he can get (which isn't saying much, with this guy's miserable luck). The second game in the series found Larry matched with his true love on a romantic, faraway isle. The latest Larry is still on the same isle. But now his wife has left him for a woman, and Larry is looking for his truer love. What will befall poor Larry next?

Simulation Games

Computers are excellent simulators of reality. Often the line blurs between simulation software labeled "games" and useful teaching tools that just happen to be computer simulations. Many computer games, especially financially-oriented ones like *Mil-lionaire* and *Tycoon*, have been harnessed into instructional devices by universities and corporations.

Hopefully, one game in particular isn't being used as a teaching aid at medical schools. *Life and Death* is the world's first interactive medical movie. All the splurting and quivering takes place at Toolworks General hospital, where you're a powerful surgeon. Your goal is to determine whether your patient lives or dies. (Aren't games supposed to provide relaxation?)

After staring at bloody body parts for hours, and being faced with the possibility of wielding the scalpel of life and death over your charge, you may be in for a little first aid yourself.

Arcade Games

This is my favorite computer game category, by far. Arcade games are easy to learn but not so easy to win. Motor skills get a workout, and they're just plain addicting.

One of the most popular games to have hit America is the first game ever to come out of the Soviet Union. The first time I saw *Tetris* was on a Macintosh. The game's crisp graphics were impressive. And the challenge of arranging falling blocks of various shapes and sizes was intensified by the Russian folk songs that played on every new level of the game. The PC version of *Tetris* shouldn't be missed, either.

WELLTRIS offers a new twist on the basic *Tetris* concept. The Soviet programmers have added three-dimensionality, so your blocks hurtle down a well where all four walls come into play. At one maddening level the programmer's face replaces Soviet street scene graphics. He seems to be smirking, since his own tiny computer screen in the background shows his high scores!

Another favorite is *Arkanoid*, now for both the IBM/Compatible and the Macintosh family of computers. Your ball hits against a paddle and eats away at various shapes, which may fall

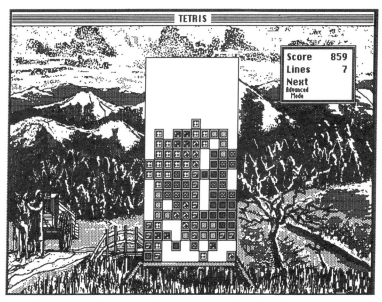

Figure 8: *Tetris combimes the sights and sounds of the U.S.S.R. with an
addictive pastime.*

and give you a goodie (like one more turn, an extra slow speed, or
missile shooting capabilities). Sounds familiar? It should, for it's
practically Pong. But the game is fun and strangely addicting. A
freeware version for the IBM/Compatibles in blazing VGA
graphics is out, and the graphics quality of the various screens is
even better—for free! This game, called *Bananoid*, was written by
a guy who just felt like experimenting with graphics. If you have
VGA, download this one from a good local Bulletin Board System.

ShufflePuck Cafe has to be one of the most nerve-racking
games around. Although it's based on the simple concept of
shufflepuck, just try beating some of these weird alien opponents.
The graphics and sound on this maddening Macintosh groaner
make it all that much more fun.

Figure 9: *Welcome to the only intergalactic shufflepuck game in town.*

Sports Software

Sports software is barely discernible from the arcade category, but you really need to get those moves down in order get going with this type of computer game. Typical of this type of game is *The Games: Summer Edition.*

Tired of your usual workout? Then it's time for a *real* challenge. Like maybe some diving, uneven parallel bars, velodrome cycling, hurdles, rings, hammer throwing, pole vaults, and a spell of archery. Now, that's for you!

Not for the quick and dirty, dive-right-in computer gamer, *The Games: Summer Edition* and other sports games like it demand repeated practice sessions and intense study of the manual. If you do take time out for the manual in *The Games: Summer Edition*, you're rewarded with "Chalk Talk" pointers, "Think Gold" tips, and memorization of the often complex key combinations or joystick moves.

Speaking of the manual, it's one of the best I've seen included with any software. A "Memorable Moments" section details some of the more obscure, interesting historical tidbits surrounding Olympics past. For example, I barely remember the time certain defeat loomed for the Czech cyclist team in Montreal, 1976 when, accidentally, all of their wheels and spare tires were picked up by garbage collectors and fed into a trash compactor. (Czech Anton Tkac captured the gold in the 1,000-meter sprint anyway, on a borrowed bike.)

And the game's educational benefits don't stop there. When you're finally ready for competition, you select one of 24 nations' flags and hear that particular national anthem. The attention to detail is superb. When I failed to maintain suitable momentum on the rings, muscle tremors and shakes racked my little man. And when my cyclist tired, a close-up displayed his face riddled with fatigue lines. After this workout, I think I feel a few fatigue lines coming on myself. Ahh, sports games.

SOURCES FOR ENTERTAINMENT SOFTWARE

Adventure Games

- *Conspiracy: the Deadlock Files*, $49.95, *Don't Go Alone*, $49.95,
  The Third Courier, $49.95 (IBM/Compatibles)
  Accolade, 550 S. Winchester Blvd., Ste. 200
  San Jose, CA 95128, (408) 985-1700

- *Gold Rush*, $49.95, *King's Quest*, $49.95
  Leisure Suit Larry in the Land of the Lounge Lizards, $49.95
  Police Quest, $49.95 (many more titles: send for catalog)
  (Apple Computers, Amiga Computers, Atari Computers,
  Commodore 64/128, IBM/Compatibles, Macintosh)
  Sierra On-Line, P.O. Box 485, Coarsegold, CA 93614, (800) 344-7448

Simulation Games

- *Ace of Aces*, $39.95 (IBM/Compatibles)
  The Cycles, $49.95 (Commodore 64/128, IBM/Compatibles)
  Eye of the Storm, $49.95 (IBM/Compatibles)

Heat Wave, $49.95 (IBM/Compatibles)
Accolade, 550 S. Winchester Blvd., Ste. 200
San Jose, CA 95128, (408) 985-1700

- *Life & Death*, $49.95 (IBM/Compatibles, Macintosh)
  Software Toolworks, One Toolworks Plaza, 13557 Ventura Blvd.
  Sherman Oaks, CA 91423, (818) 907-6789

- *Baron*, $49.95, *Millionaire II*, $49.95
  Tycoon, $49.95 (IBM/Compatibles)
  Blue Chip Software, 185 Berry St.
  San Francisco, CA 94107, (415) 546-1866

ARCADE GAMES

- *Arkanoid*, $37.95 (IBM/Compatibles, Macintosh)
  Taito Software, Inc., 267 W. Esplanade, Ste. 206
  North Vancouver, BC V7M 1A5, Canada

- *Shufflepuck Cafe*, $39.95 (Macintosh)
  Broderbund Software, 17 Paul Dr.
  San Rafael, CA 94903-2101, (415) 492-3200

- *Tetris*, $49.95 (IBM/Compatibles, Macintosh)
  Spectrum HoloByte, 2061 Challenger Dr.
  Alameda, CA 94501, (415) 522-1164

- *WELLTRIS*, $49.95 (IBM/Compatibles)
  Spectrum HoloByte, 2061 Challenger Dr.
  Alameda, CA 94501, (415) 522-3584

SPORTS SOFTWARE

- *California Games*, $39.95, *Games: Summer*, $49.95
  Games: Winter, $49.95, *Sporting News Baseball*, $39.95
  (many more titles; send for catalog)
  (Apple Computers, Commodore 64/128, IBM/Compatibles)
  Epyx, P.O. Box 6041
  Sherman Oaks, CA 91413

- *HardBall II*, $39.95 (IBM/Compatibles)
  Accolade, 550 S. Winchester Blvd., Ste. 200
  San Jose, CA 95128, (408) 985-1700

CHAPTER 5

A Computer in the Garden

A computer in the garden? The image of mud-encrusted floppy disks comes to mind, but a computer can be just as essential to the garden as a shovel or hose is. Specialty gardening software programs have made America's favorite hobby easier and more enjoyable for beginners and "green thumbs" alike.

By integrating familiar computer programs like spreadsheets, databases, Gantt charts, and even word processors, gardening programs give a boost to the gardener's organizational abilities. Today's gardening software can do everything from helping the new gardener plot enough rows of corn to assisting the landscaper in selecting a compact shrub with bronze foliage and red blossoms. Whatever your gardening interests, a computer can maximize your gardening time and effort—leaving *you* more time to (what else?) smell the roses.

TASKS FOR GARDENING SOFTWARE

- Plant or Crop Selection
- Row/Plot Planning
- Timing Plantings
- Scheduling Gardening Tasks
- Keeping Garden Records

- Printing Out Seed Orders
- Botanical Reference Guide

Plant or Crop Selection

One of the most difficult, yet enjoyable, gardening tasks involves neither rake nor shovel and seldom requires bending over: deciding what to plant. The fun part is pouring over the full-color seed catalogs, savoring each plant's description while picturing your garden overflowing with magnificent flowers and succulent vegetables. But most people have limited garden space, and narrowing down the plant wish list is a cruel but necessary job.

After the usual method of going through the seed catalogue and writing down every bush with blue flowers, then going back to pick out just those with dark green foliage, and then narrowing down *that* list to just the drought-tolerant bushes, you'll probably give up and pour concrete, instead. (Don't do it.) Every gardening program contains a plant database to make plant selection a snap.

Before your computer selects plants for your garden, the program asks where you live, when you'll be planting, and other particulars. You'll be asked some questions that help the computer customize the program for your region, garden size, preference for rows or beds, north/south or east/west orientation, and the like. Many programs ask you for your zip code, so you don't accidentally choose a frost-needy fruit tree for a Southern California garden. Others, such as Jasmine Software's California-oriented *Plant Perfect*, focus on plants suited to a particular region.

(Note: When you've answered the program's questions about your garden, you'll be asked to give that garden setup a name. The program will then save all your information to disk under that filename, giving you a record of the garden for posterity.)

Selecting plants to meet a set of requirements is simply a matter of typing in your specifications, such as bushes, blue flowers, dark foliage or drought-resistant. The gardening software does a rapid search of its database, and displays a list of the plants fitting your criteria. Then type in each of the plants on this list, have the program do a search, and get ready to learn more about its cultural requirements.

Figure 10: *Garden software databases are informative and easy to use.*

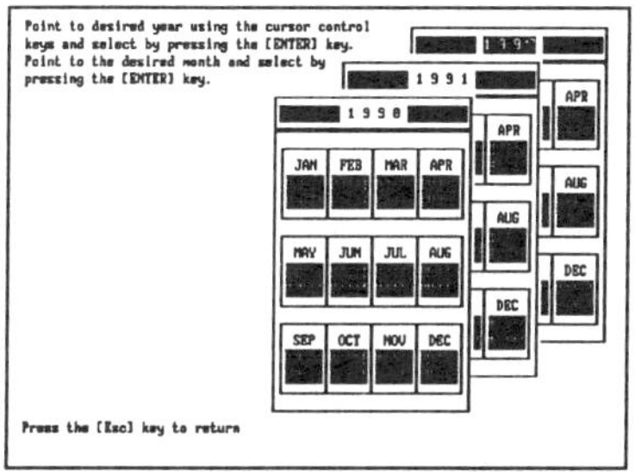

Figure 11: *Garden schedulers make you stick to a plan, and your garden will love you for it.*

Plant database sizes vary from program to program. So do the types of plants the databases contain. *Plant Perfect* has over 1,100 tree/shrub, ornamental and fruit/vegetable listings. *Ortho's Computerized Gardening*'s database contains 750 ornamentals. *Garden Manager* comes with 167 vegetables listed, with room for a total of 200. Two other gardening programs also allow you to add your own favorites. *CompuGarden* lists 80 vegetables, herbs, and flowers, with room for 125 varieties. And *Gardener's Assistant* offers 55 vegetables; 45 more can be added. All of the programs allow modification of the database entries.

Row/Plot Planning

Most people suspect that a plant's minimal light, food, and water requirements must be met in order for it to thrive. But there is a fourth factor to be considered: space. When deprived of sufficient room to grow, a plant is deprived of all those other requirements and suffers stress.

Stress can effect a plant in several ways, none of which will add to the beauty or bounty of your garden. Plant responses to stress range from poor growth, premature defoliation, and scrawny flowers and fruits, to production of low-vitality seeds. Although questions of yield and fruit quality pertain mostly to the vegetable/fruit garden, ornamentals have space requirements too.

By using gardening software you can properly allocate every square inch of space. Once you've selected plants from the software's database, the program will ask how much you want to grow (or how many people you want to feed, in the case of vegetables). The program then goes to work, placing plants according to height, cultural requirements, and tolerance for neighboring plants.

Several gardening programs will draw the layout on the screen, and you can print it out for later reference. (The printout is easier than the monitor to take to your garden site too.)

Timing Plantings

The worst thing a garden can have is patches of bare soil, unplanted, unloved. Besides being ugly, fallow corners promote weed growth and soil erosion. And you could be getting flowers or vegetables out of that space.

Gardening software enables you to take full advantage of the space you have by planning when to start seedlings, transplant, thin within the rows, and harvest. Once you harvest, *Compu-Garden* times up to four successive plantings—maximizing your garden's output. This program also offers another plus: it keeps track of each plant's location each year, automatically rotating that crop to another location the following year. Crop rotation is important. Even in a small garden it helps to curb disease and minimize the depletion of soil nutrients.

The beginning gardener can also benefit by learning what plants do better in what season. The database entry for eggplant indicates that, being a summer annual, spring sowing is advised.

Scheduling Gardening Tasks

The road to hell is paved with good intentions, and that goes double for the garden, which seems to have a mind of its own if left to its own devices. Even though you know what needs to be done, and intend to do it soon, you might forget or put off the task too long. Plants seem to go by their own timetable, and without a regular program of weeding, mulching, watering, planting, and seed starting, the garden can get out of hand quicker than you'd think. Why not let your computer keep you organized?

Soil Building With a Computer

The most sure-fire method for improving your soil's humus content is taken directly from commercial organic farmers. Cover cropping, or "green manure," is provided by sowing a quick-growing crop and digging it into the ground before it matures—when it will provide the greatest bulk, and yet not be too tall to turn under. Since the best time to plant a cover crop is between clearing away one crop and planting another, let your computer schedule in a crop of green manure between the tomatoes and the winter broccoli. If you live in a colder climate with one main growing season, why not start a hearty cover crop at summer's end instead of letting the land go fallow?

Most gardening software provides planting timetables. Garden Manager *produces a weekly garden schedule to which you can add tasks, such as planting green manure.*

Cheap seed and quick growth makes for the best cover crop to plant. Just broadcast one ounce of seed per square yard, rake it in, and water regularly (in dryer climates). Vetches and cow peas from the legume family fix nitrogen in the soil—an added benefit. Other good green manures are sweet clover, alfalfa, mustard, and winter rye. And if your neighbors look askance at your thriving alfalfa "lawn," just tell them you're teaching the children about agriculture!

Gardening software uses the information you enter in the plant selection module to calculate your garden schedule. Based on the last frost date in your area, *Garden Manager* will indicate planting date, weeks for plant maturation, and weeks of harvest. You can view or print as many weeks as you wish. *CompuGarden* lets you view and print two types of planting schedules. A Gantt chart maps out the entire season's activities and shows when to start seeds in flats or beds, transplant, thin, fertilize, and harvest each crop. A weekly schedule summarizes tasks you need to accomplish each week. Both programs let you individualize the tasks.

Keeping Garden Records

Remembering the outstanding plant varieties of gardens past is easy. Every gardener can rattle off the name of the rose that produced dozens of blooms or the one cucumber that never succumbed to mildew. But who remembers the failures?

With the aid of gardening software, the computer can help you record all the varieties you try, good and not so good, so you don't get stuck with a mediocre variety again. You can then use this information to modify and personalize the plant database in future years.

Journal modules allow you to record data about the weather or unusual insect activity during a particular season as well. Or anything else you feel is important. The journal module in *Compu-Garden* has a separate productivity log area, where you assign a market value to each of the crops you grow. The program will then calculate the net value of your season's effort, subtracting labor, materials, and any other costs incurred. Many gardeners won't want to use this feature!

Gardening software allows you to print the various schedules, plant selections, garden plans, and database entries included in the program. Computers excel at generating records, and the value of being able to go back and see where the beans went last year is incalculable for accurately rotating your crops.

Printing Seed Orders

Buying seeds at the local nursery or discount store can be chancy—you might not find a very good selection of varieties, and you don't know how fresh the seeds are. Getting seed catalogues in the mail is fun. Reading seed catalogue descriptions and cultural notes offers a great gardening education too. And they're almost always free. The computer has helped you plan the garden and select your varieties, but now you have to go back and forth between your favorite seed catalogues and your variety printout to order your seeds. One program, *Garden Manager*, does away with the tedium involved in seed ordering.

While choosing what crops you want to plant, *Garden Manager* lets you identify with a two-letter code what seed company carries that plant. You can then print separate variety lists sorted for each seed company, making the ordering process effortless. This list includes the number of plants you planned to grow, which helps in deciding how much seed of any one variety to buy.

Botanical Reference Guide

The database components of gardening programs are invaluable sources of information, particularly those programs offering larger databases. Sorting for different plant characteristics is easy with a computer. Most programs let you search by botanical and common names. But what if you forget a plant's name? *Ortho's Computerized Gardening* lets you use an asterisk to indicate that there are letters missing either before or after the typed letters. If you place an asterisk after a portion of a name, the selector chooses all the plants that begin with those letters. Conversely, you can place an asterisk before a portion of a name, and the plant selector will make a list of all the plant names containing those letters anywhere in the name.

HIGH AND LOW POINTS

On the minus side, *Ortho's Computerized Gardening* doesn't take full advantage of the computer's power. The landscape planner is a large piece of glossy grid paper, and a plant shopping list also comes on "hardcopy." The plant selector database leaves out vegetables, so a vegetable planting guide is included—in the form of a poster. You can't add plants to the database, or modify existing listings. And if you need instructions on feeding requirements, spacing, pest susceptibilities, or how deep to plant, you'll have to consult the 192-page Ortho *Gardening Techniques* book tucked into the package.

The program is primarily a plant database—and an excellent one. This is a great program for people interested in landscaping. The calculator, which you can access from anywhere in the program, and notepad are thoughtful additions.

Plant Perfect functions solely as a database. Topping the list at over 1,100 entries, this is a great reference tool. But since the entries are all mild-winter varieties, people in northern climates are better off with one of the other programs.

Even though *Gardener's Assistant*'s main strength is garden layout, it plots the garden in single rows, which is useless for people with small gardens or those who prefer beds. And if you choose too much of one vegetable for your garden size while selecting plants, *all* of your plant choices are wiped out—and you're zapped back to the main menu.

On the other hand, *CompuGarden* bases all its plantings on 4-foot wide raised beds. Even though raised beds are an excellent way to go, especially if you have clay soil, it would be nice to have a choice in the matter. Every garden (and gardener) is different. In light of *CompuGarden*'s all-around superiority in this software category, however, this is a small drawback.

Computerized Composting

We all know that composting garden refuse is a good thing, but who remembers to turn their compost heaps regularly? Let your computer's scheduling abilities remind you. The simplest compost heap can be formed by taking enough 36-inch cement wire to form a circle 3 feet wide, and joining the ends. Just layer your chopped-up leaves, weeds, vines, grass clippings, prunings, and other garden refuse inside with soil and a little manure. Sprinkle the layers with a small amount of water as you build.

If you take the wire apart, re-form the circle nearby, and pile the heap back inside ("turning" the heap) at least every week, you'll get rich, clean compost in only weeks. The more you turn the pile, the hotter it gets and the quicker it decomposes. Your plants will smile at the sight of you coming over to mulch them with computer-generated compost.

ALTERNATIVES TO GARDENING SOFTWARE

Your computer can work in your garden even if you don't own specialty gardening software. Conventional word processors, spreadsheets, and databases can be used to keep journals, plot plots, count costs, and even print address labels—for those who can't resist those luscious seed catalogues. And the national on-line service Compuserve offers The Good Earth special interest group, where a gardening forum allows members to exchange tips and questions, as well as member-written gardening programs.

SOURCES FOR GARDENING SOFTWARE

- *Plant Perfect* (IBM/Compatible) $65.00, (Apple II) $65.00
  Jasmine Software, Inc., 3359 Karen Ave.
  Long Beach, CA 90808, (213) 496-3376

- *CompuGarden*, $69.95 (IBM/Compatible)
  CompuGarden, Inc., 1006 Highland Dr.
  Silver Spring, MD 20910, (301) 587-7995

- *The Gardener's Assistant* (IBM/Compatible) $45.00
  (Apple II) $39.95, (Commodore) $29.95
  Shannon Software, Ltd., P.O. Box 6126
  Falls Church, VA 22046, (703) 573-9274

- *Ortho's Computerized Gardening*
  (IBM/Compatible) $49.95 (Apple II) $49.95
  (Commodore) $49.95 (Mac Plus) $49.95
  Ortho Information Services, 575 Market St.
  San Francisco, CA 94105

- *Garden Manager*, $49.95 (IBM/Compatible)
  Jeff Ball and Gary Gack, P.O. Box 338
  Springfield, PA 19064

- CompuServe Information Services
  P.O. Box 202012, 500 Arlington Center Blvd.
  Columbus, OH 43220, (800) 848-8199, (614) 457-8600

PART THREE

CHAPTER 6

Health and Nutrition on Your Home Computer

The words "health" and "computer" probably live in separate areas of your brain. When asked to picture a computer user, odds are a pale, unkempt, out-of-shape guy or gal with a greenish smile comes to mind. Yet a new breed of health-oriented computer software can dash those old stereotypes. After all, keeping healthy involves staying organized, and the computer is certainly fit in that area.

Diet and nutrition software contain extensive databases to help keep tabs on your food consumption for the day. The software makes use of your computer's math abilities to calculate total intake of calories, fats, vitamins, and other nutrients. If you're forced to say "diet," some programs include motivational essays to get you psyched up for a new physique.

But, before you can analyze it, you have to prepare and eat it. That's where food preparation software comes in. The culinary arts take on a new, high-tech appeal with the many cuisine software packages on the market. (No, cheese puffs are not the primary ingredient in each recipe.)

And you never have to worry about serving the proper beverage when your computer acts as your wine steward and bartender. Wine and cocktail selection are simple and fun with the proper software. And you'll find that wine goes with so many more things than Jolt Cola ever did.

Although it's no substitute for a doctor, your computer, loaded with stress monitoring software, can help you head off any poor health habits. Exercise is a perfect stress reducer, and the right software can keep track of those laps swum, or miles jogged or biked, too.

TASKS FOR HEALTH AND NUTRITION SOFTWARE

- Monitor Your Diet and Calorie Intake
- Create Gourmet Specialties
- Choose Appropriate Wines and Cocktails
- Keep an Eye on Stress and Poor Health Habits
- Diagnose Simple Health Disorders
- Organize Your Exercise Schedule/Track Your Workouts

DIET AND NUTRITION SOFTWARE

Typical of programs in this category is one for the IBM/Compatible family of computers called *Munch. Munch* asks you to input all the foods you eat throughout the day. The program then analyzes their caloric and nutritive values, based on the Exchange System. Developed by the American Diabetes Association, the Exchange System divides foods into six basic lists or exchanges: milk, vegetable, fruit, bread/starches, meat, and fat. Within each group, the foods contain roughly equal amounts of protein, carbohydrates, fat, and calories—thus you can *exchange* one for another.

Munch's main menu lists 12 exchanges. The other six exchanges result from the program dividing the meat/dairy exchange into low, medium, and high fat groups. Additional categories come from fun-, combination-, and free-food exchanges.

Say you choose an exchange like milk. *Munch* asks you to enter the number of 1-cup servings of milk, yogurt, or sour cream you've consumed that day. Although the manual advertises the program's ability to accept fractional amounts, this pertains only to amounts over the one-serving minimum—so I didn't enter the 1/4-cup of milk I add to my morning coffee. Another drawback is trying to mentally note your servings of each exchange member until you've scanned the entire list and entered the total. It would be easier to flag each food as you come to it and have the program keep a running total.

At the end of each exchange, the screen tells you how many grams of nutrients and calories have gone down your gullet. You get a similar report after entering all the day's exchanges, along with a short recommendation for balancing your intake. After spitting out a 1135 calorie total composed of 17 percent Fun Foods, one day's report admonished me: "Small percentage or nothing from this group usually results in better nutritional intake." Sadly, there's no way nerds can adjust this module.

That daily report can be printed or saved by labeling with a date. A history printout averages all the saved reports. *Munch*'s reports are a bit on the sparse side, however. I was told that my intake of 1135 calories for the day was 27 percent below the 1557 calories a person of my age, dimensions, and activity level should consume. Yet nowhere was listed a goal to which a person of my build could aspire. Another program, *Food Processor II*, lets you enter the specifics for your current weight or for your goal weight, giving you a better idea about how to reach that goal. This program goes into detail on vitamins, trace minerals and the like, and includes an extensive reference book.

Whatever the drawbacks, this program and others like it force you to examine and record your intake. This leads to guilt and self-loathing, feelings that are natural to dieting.

On the shareware front, *MealMate* lets you enter a given food, a whole recipe, or an entire meal. After a run through its huge database, it spits out the nutritional lowdown. The program contains such scale-tippers as Camembert cheese and angel food cake. But those with truly gourmand tendencies can use the append feature to add favorites that *MealMate*'s programmers missed.

If all this database measuring forces you to take some measures of your own, a shareware program for IBM/Compatibles called *Weight Control* is packed with motivational utilities. These programs can test your dieting skills via questionnaire, calculate your average weight loss over a period of dieting, and more. The program features essays on why you shouldn't fear dieting. Included is a diet shopping list complete with caloric values.

Another good program, *Managing Your Food*, lets you plan your shopping list according to nutritional values *and* cost.

The Diet Balancer contains the usual features, but with an added plus: This program lets you plug in your exercise or fitness program. We all know exercise is the only real way to get into shape—combined with small portions of healthy food, of course. This program features graphic screens that make it easy to see imbalances in your nutritive intake.

East Meets West Nutrition Planner, from the Japanese-specialty publishers Ishi Press, asks you to record every meal you eat for a year. The program lets you save an oft-repeated meal under a label, such as "Egg Breakfast," allowing you to plug in the meal as a whole, rather than as separate food entries.

The fast-food diehards will appreciate *Fast Food Calculator* for the Macintosh. The thoughtful folks at Heizer Software have published a HyperCard stack that provides nutrition and ingredient information for major fast food chains—complete with *speech* capabilities. Sounds scary. Luckily your stomach doesn't have speech capabilities after a fast-food feast.

CUISINE PREPARATION SOFTWARE

"What's for grub?" The familiar refrain greets you every evening, no matter how harried or hassled your day's been. Unfortunately, the answer often may be less than inspired. Why not let the computer help you plan and execute meals? The many cuisine preparation software packages available provide new ideas for familiar ingredients or can suggest new foods with which to experiment.

If you enjoy browsing through good cookbooks, cuisine software's searching abilities can let you explore particular foods or methods in depth. *Great Chefs of PBS*, for most computer systems, even includes biographies on famous chefs. If everybody considers *you* a world class chef, you'll find recipe programs that let you file, sort, and retrieve your own indispensable master-pieces. And many of the cuisine disks allow you to add your own creations.

The computer's organizational abilities can help you revitalize family dinners, but why not enlist its help in planning a surprise dinner party? The ability to flag various dishes as you browse, then save them to a "Tonight's Menu" file, is one of *Dinner at Eight*'s best features. And cuisine software often offers modules to assist in shopping as well as chopping. Most of the *Micro Kitchen Companion* software will re-size recipes for up to 999 guests— which does away with risky and tedious recipe multiplication tasks.

If the smell of bread baking in the oven is too much to resist, a shareware offering for IBM/Compatibles can offer mouth-water-ing, fragrant creations in an instant. *Computer Baker* lets you choose between 99 recipes from six categories: snacks, fudge and candy, muffins and biscuits, cookies, cakes and frostings, and pies. The documentation even defines the word "homemade" as "made from scratch" (for those who have been sitting in front of a computer a little too long).

If keying all your favorite recipes into one of these cuisine programs sounds like more trouble than it's worth, *Recipe Index System* lets you enter the principle ingredients of each recipe. The program then searches through that index to locate the names and locations of recipes containing those ingredients. Commonly used by people with large cookbook collections, this program could be applied to index other items—such as the contents of storage boxes.

WINE AND COCKTAIL SELECTION SOFTWARE

Sometimes you get the urge to do it yourself, no matter how complex, time-consuming, or intricate the task may be. When that urge hits, brew some beer! Now you can get that blend of hops, malt, and grain just right. Two HyperCard stacks for the Macintosh, *Homebrew* and *Brew Records*, contain step-by-step directions on brewing your own beer.

Although it's not as good a listener as Joe the bartender down at the neighborhood pub, your computer will never kick you out at 2 a.m. Programs specializing in mixology (bartending to you and me) let you wow your friends and sample new and exotic drinks at the press of a key. A plus with the shareware program *PC-Bartender* is that it keeps an inventory of your liquor cabinet and knows in advance whether or not you have all the ingredients for that triple mocha sideswiper your wiseguy guest has ordered.

On the other hand, if you have too much of that slim-price vodka sitting around, the program can sort for ways to use it up. The program's database contains hundreds of exotic and yummy drink recipes.

Another electronic barkeep, *Official Mr. Boston Micro Bartender's Guide Deluxe*, runs on every type of computer. This classic, converted to disk, contains a staggering [pun intended] 1,000 recipes, plus a listing of wine and beer selections. A VIP party-planning module lets you pick the drinks your guests enjoy most and will even prepare a shopping list right down to the correct glassware. You can re-size recipes for up to 999 guests (but you better have a huge punchbowl).

The *Micro Wine Companion* series of programs is available for almost every computer operating system. These programs are fun to use and add a touch of high-tech savvy to any meal. You can even pull up a chart of your cavernous wine cellar. Thousands of brands, labels, and vintners are included, so you'll never make a *faux pour* again.

STRESS AND PREVENTIVE MEDICINE SOFTWARE

Cholesterol is a common concern among health conscious Americans. We have slowly come to realize that we can't shove fatty, nutrient-void foods down our throats forever without some kind of toll on our systems. Two programs for IBM/Compatible computers help monitor cholesterol intake. Alternatives to killer foods are suggested in a non-nagging way.

Take Control of Cholesterol, based on the bestseller *Eater's Choice* by Doctors Ron and Nancy Goor, offers a way to systematize your fight against cholesterol. After undergoing the program's questionnaire, the system determines your ideal intake of saturated fats. Using this information and your own dietary likes and dislikes, it helps you plan healthful menus using 200 recipes and 1,700 foods. It tracks your actual intake and helps find less lethal alternatives. A pop-up Dietary Ledger feature makes it easier to monitor your progress. A superior feature offered by *Take Charge of Your Cholesterol* is the on-screen running total of all the cholesterol and calories you've accumulated since the first day of your diet.

The 8-Week Cholesterol Cure is based on, and comes with, the well-known bestseller of the same name. Charts from the book help you input the ideal number of calories you must consume and the cholesterol level you must maintain daily. The acid test comes after comparing your ideal daily cholesterol and caloric needs with your actual food intake. The Daily Analysis section is firm but kind, giving you better alternatives in case you're not meeting your goals.

Some foods just don't agree with us. Food allergies and sensitivities can be hard to pin down, however, because we usually combine many foods at mealtimes. Your computer is a perfect tool

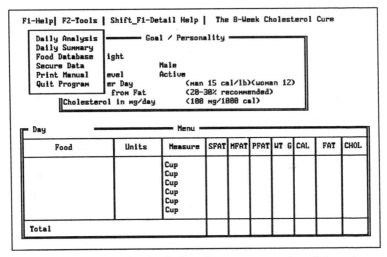

Figure 12: Cholesterol tracking is effortless when your computer does all the work.

to help isolate those ingredients that aren't your cup of tea. *Well-Aware Food Sensitivity Software* helps you spot the foods to which you have allergies, then plans nutritious balanced menus with the foods that make you feel good.

An entire health database is offered by the *Expert Express: Your Health* software program for the IBM/Compatible family of computers. The program provides instant access to a 350-page knowledge base of health information from the U.S. Government. If you have children, or a hypochondriacal partner, a medical advisory software package might be handy to have around the house. These programs have you answer a series of questions, then progressively narrow down the possible maladies. *FamilyCare Software*, for IBM/Compatible and Macintosh computers, is modeled upon the diagnostic process used by doctors to help parents with their children's medical problems. A shareware program, *Parents Home Companion: Managing Colic*, provides parents and those responsible for childcare with expert assistance in a range of common problems. An "artificial intelligence" scheme lets your answers guide you to new question banks.

Another shareware program aptly titled *"Pregnant"* helps women with unstable menstrual cycles track the times when they are most fertile. The program takes into account age, physical characteristics, and the dates of each menstrual cycle. The program demands some effort on your part: Daily body temperatures dating back to the last two months must be faithfully recorded. The screen displays the average length and stability of the menstrual cycle and the period of ovulation. Don't blame your computer if a little bundle of joy arrives accidentally, though!

On the more cerebral side, *Stress and Shrink*, a group of shareware programs, flags any dangerous mental imbalances you might be experiencing. One of the programs takes you through the Holmes Life Change Index, that infamous list of the 43 most stress, provoking life events liable to take you right over the deep end if you're not careful. In one particular session with the program I answered "yes" to every question. *Stress* rated my stress level at 1443 (compared to *what*?) and exclaimed, "Your score indicates you have had major life changes." Duh.

Shrink, on the same shareware disk, asks you to list your preferences in many realms and then pigeonholes you neatly into one of four personality types. Another shareware offering called *Health Risk* evaluates your exposure to environmental and hereditary perils such as pollution, smoke, or lousy cooking.

A program called *PC-Relax* offers shapes and colors at which you can gaze in order to relieve stress and eye fatigue. Or, try a public domain fractals program if you have an IBM/Compatible system equipped with an EGA/VGA monitor. You'll be reminded of the lightshow-saturated concerts of the late 60s (or perhaps a paisley necktie, depending on your age).

EXERCISE MONITORING SOFTWARE

Electronic devices for monitoring your workouts are common. Why buy yet another clumsy, expensive gadget when you already own a perfect tool for the job? Computer software can make sure you're getting an optimum workout, whatever way you choose to sweat.

Before you start any exercise regime, assess your overall readiness for strenuous activity with *Physical Fitness Evaluation.* The program evaluates strength, flexibility, endurance, foot type and body composition, and analyzes your overall fitness. For the IBM/Compatible family of computers, *Personal Fitness Planner* lets you develop an optimal activity and caloric input plan. If you're beginning a fitness program after being sedentary or ill, there's a software package for the Apple series of computers called *Rehabilitation Fitness Evaluation* that will let you ease into a more active lifestyle.

MacFanatics will enjoy pumping with *MacMuscle.* This program generates schedules based on your muscle group selection and provides animated introductions to chosen exercises.

Cyclists with Macs or IBM/Compatibles can benefit from *Biking Calorie Counter*, which calculates tables for "gear inches," miles-per-hour, and calories burned per workout. Runners will appreciate *Graphic Coach*'s ability to display each run graphically. The program calculates the pace for each training and racing day. It can present all your runs in monthly or yearly tables and can calculate and display a specific training schedule for the next week based on your most recent 5K or 10K race elapsed time. The schedule, based on calculated aerobic capacities, maximizes your training effort.

SOURCES FOR HEALTH AND NUTRITION SOFTWARE

Diet and Nutrition Software

- *Munch*, $39.95 (IBM/Compatibles)
  C.R. Smolin, 7760 Fay Ave., Ste. J
  La Jolla, CA 92037, (619) 454-3404

- *Food Processor II*, $250.00
  (Apple Computers, IBM/Compatibles, Macintosh)
  ESHA Research, P.O. Box 13028
  Salem, OR 97309, (503) 585-6242

- *MealMate* (Disk #700) (IBM/Compatibles)
  PC-SIG, 1030 East Duane Avenue, Ste. D
  Sunnyvale, CA 94086, (800) 222-2996 (CA)
  (800) 245-6717 (USA), (408) 730-9291

- *MacNutriplan*, $75.00 (Macintosh)
  187 Gardiners Ave.
  Levittoun, NY 11756, (800) 535-3438

- *Nutritionist II*, $295.00, *Nutritionist III*, $495.00
  (Apple Computers, Macintosh)
  N-Squared Computing, 5318 Forest Ridge Rd.
  Silverton, OR 97381, (503) 873-5906

- *Nutri-fax*, $59.95 (Commodore Amiga Computer)
  Meggido Enterprises, P.O. Box 3020-191-A02
  Riverside, CA 92159, (714) 683-5666

- *Weight Control* (Disk #1325)
  Managing Your Food (Disk #1056), (IBM/Compatibles)
  PC-SIG, 1030 East Duane Avenue, Ste. D
  Sunnyvale, CA 94086, (800) 222-2996 (CA)
  (800) 245-6717 (USA), (408) 730-9291

- *The Diet Balancer*, $59.95 (IBM/Compatibles)
  Nutridata Software Corp., P.O. Box 769
  Wappingers Falls, NY 12590
  (914) 298-1308, (800) 289-1157

- *East Meets West Nutrition Planner*, $49.95 (IBM/Compatibles)
  Ishi Press International, 1400 N. Shoreline Blvd. A7
  Mountain View, CA 94043

- *Fast Food Calculator*, $15.00 (Macintosh)
  Heizer Software, 1941 Oak Park Blvd., Ste. 30
  Pleasant Hill, CA 94523, (415) 943-7667

- *Fast Food Micro-Guide*, $49.00 (Apple Computers)
  Learning Seed Co., 330 Telser Rd.
  Lake Zurich, IL 60047, (312) 540-8855

Cuisine Preparation Software

- *Micro Kitchen Companion*, $39.95
  Great Chefs of PBS Series, $24.95
  (Apple Computers, IBM/Compatibles, Macintosh)
  Lifestyle Publishing Group, 63 Orange St.
  St. Augustine, FL 32084, (800) 525-4653

- *Dinner at Eight*, $49.95, *Encore Edition*, $15.95 (Macintosh)
  Rubicon Publishing, 2111 Dickson Dr., Ste. 30
  Austin, TX 78704

- *Computer Baker* (Disk #1171)
  Recipe Index System (Disk #1317), (IBM/Compatibles)
  PC-SIG, 1030 East Duane Avenue, Ste. D
  Sunnyvale, CA 94086, (800) 222-2996 (CA)
  (800) 245-6717 (USA), (408) 730-9291

Wine and Cocktail Selection Software

- *Homebrew*, $15.00 (Macintosh)
  Heizer Software, 1941 Oak Park Blvd., Ste. 30
  Pleasant Hill, CA 94523, (415) 943-7667

- *PC-Bartender* (Disk #1213), (IBM/Compatibles)
  PC-SIG, 1030 East Duane Avenue, Ste. D
  Sunnyvale, CA 94086, (800) 222-2996 (CA)
  (800) 245-6717 (USA), (408) 730-9291

- *Mr. Boston's Official Micro Bartender's Guide*, $19.49
  Micro Wine Companion, $49.95, *World of Wine* Series, $14.95
  (Apple Computers, Atari Computers, Commodore 64/128,
  IBM/Compatibles, Macintosh)
  Lifestyle Publishing Group, 63 Orange St.
  St. Augustine, FL 32084, (800) 525-4653

Stress and Preventive Medicine Software

- *Take Control of Cholesterol*, $49.95 (IBM/Compatibles)
  Lifestyle Publishing Group, 63 Orange St.
  St. Augustine, FL 32084, (800) 525-4653

- *The 8-Week Cholesterol Cure*, $39.95 (IBM/Compatibles)
  Disk-Count Software, 1751 W. Country Rd. B, #107
  St. Paul, MN 55113, (800) 331-6902

- *Expert Express: Your Health*, $39.95 (IBM/Compatibles)
  Professional Knowledge Systems, Inc., P.O. Box 11683
  St. Louis, MO 63105, (800) 727-1510

- *Family Medical Advisor*, $39.95 (IBM/Compatibles)
  Navic Software, 5606 PGA Blvd., Ste. 211
  Palm Beach Gardens, FL 33418, (407) 622-3715

- *Familycare Software*, $99.00 (IBM/Compatibles, Macintosh)
  Lundin Laboratories, Inc., 29451 Greenfield Rd.
  Southfield, MI 48076, (800) 426-8426

- *Pregnant* (Disk #1325), (IBM/Compatibles)
  PC-SIG, 1030 East Duane Avenue, Ste. D
  Sunnyvale, CA 94086, (800) 222-2996 (CA)
  (800) 245-6717 (USA), (408) 730-9291

- *PC-Relax*, $39.95 (IBM/Compatibles)
  Tru-Image, P.O. Box 660
  Cooper Station, New York, NY 10276, (212) 777-7609

- *Stress & Shrink* (Disk #074), *Health Risk* (Disk #331), (IBM/Compatibles)
  California Freeware, 1747 E. Ave. Q, Unit C-1
  Palmdale, CA 93550, (805) 273-0300

- *Stress Management 2*, $49.95
  Total Stress Management System, $100.00
  (Apple Computers, IBM/Compatibles)
  Psychological Psoftware, 312 Los Altos Dr.
  Aptos, CA 95003, (408) 688-6808

Exercise Monitoring Software

- *MacMuscle*, $64.95 (Macintosh)
  Tech 2000 Software, Inc., 530 Franklyn Ave.
  Indialantic, FL 32903, (407) 727-8815

- *Biking Calorie Counter*, $4.00 (IBM/Compatibles, Macintosh)
  Heizer Software, 1941 Oak Park Blvd., Ste. 30
  Pleasant Hill, CA 94523, (415) 943-7667

- *Graphic Coach*, $24.95 (IBM/Compatibles)
  Dunnigan Designs, 3536 Utah St.
  San Diego, CA 92104, (619) 299-0752

- *Physical Fitness Evaluation*, $39.95 (IBM/Compatibles)
  Wholebody Health Management, 18653 Ventura Blvd., Ste. 137
  Tarzana, CA 91356, (818) 708-2735

- *Personal Fitness Planner*, $49.95 (IBM/Compatibles)
  Occidental Computer Systems, Inc., 8100 Balboa Blvd.
  Van Nuys, CA 91406, (818) 786-9920

- *Rehabilitation Fitness Evaluation*, $39.95 (Apple Computers)
  Wholebody Health Management, 18653 Ventura Blvd., Ste. 137
  Tarzana, CA 91356, (818) 708-2735

CHAPTER 7

Personal Growth Software

Computers seem so rigid and mechanical—and they are. After all, they're only electronic devices. People usually peg the computer as a tool to promote productivity, yet the home computer can help folks get more out of life in other, less tangible ways. If some of your goals include working on personal growth and inner development, you'll find your home computer a great ally.

Computers can help you get in touch with yourself by focusing your attention inward. Your computer and you have something in common: it's fascinated by you and everything about you. It never tires of hearing about your life, your dreams, your aspirations. It can prod you to focus on your strengths in order to create a winning resume—even when you're unemployed without a friend in the world. What's more, the privacy of your home computer guarantees that no one will laugh if you get the urge to try out "silly" pursuits like handwriting analysis or astrology. And you'll find that your computer will comfort you in matters of the heart, once it's loaded with the proper software.

Creativity is hard to pin down. But your computer's organizing skills and artificial intelligence capabilities can help make creativity more a habit than a bolt from the blue. And the many

I-Ching, numerology, and even tarot software programs around can transform your computer screen into a window on the mysterious world of symbols and signs. Whether these programs are used for sheer laughs or in earnest depends on you, but they definitely put home computing in another dimension.

RESUME SOFTWARE

Writing a resume that's memorable without being boastful takes some doing. Computer software designed to make you reflect on your accomplishments and qualifications can make a rough job a little easier, however. Resumes that get, and hold, employers' attention demand the organization that only your home computer can provide.

A software package for the IBM/Compatible family of computers combines resume creation with an entire job search strategy. *The Resume Kit* provides several on-screen templates to get you going. The forms are already organized, and you just fill them in with the particulars of your experience, education, skills, and interests. Once you're familiar with what goes where, customizing your resume is easy. Different resume styles can be selected depending on whether you're still a student, changing careers, or seeking a career in business, computer science, or academia. The program automatically adjusts fonts and works with dot-matrix or laser printers (the latter looks way better).

Perhaps the strongest feature of this program is the manual, which is packed full of interview tips, job hunting strategies, and more. For example, the manual emphasizes writing a thank-you letter after an interview: a crucial piece of advice ignored all too often.

A helpful appendix containing action words will help you add pizazz to your job descriptions. Additional resources, and even a sample cover letter, are included as well. *The Resume Kit* contains other essential job hunting aids, such as a word processor for writing cover letters, equipped with a 100,000 word spell checker.

An on-screen calendar ensures that you'll keep track of appointments and follow-ups despite the frenzy and disorientation you may be experiencing. The program has a clean feel to it with endless helpful menus and dialog boxes.

There's one additional, amazing feature to this honey of a program. *The Resume Kit* comes with an offer for a free, four-month listing of your resume on the International Business Network on-line career advancement network. The documentation claims that IBN (hmmm, sounds like . . .) is used by companies to fill thousands of positions each year. Whether these claims are true or not, every little bit helps when you're advancing your career.

On the shareware front, a program called *Apply* helps keep track of applications you've sent out for jobs, contests, grants, dream dates—you name it. *Apply* works as a mini-database, storing the pertinent data and merging it with text files. You can keep records of past encounters with specific institutions, as well as printing out letters, resumes, and envelopes. Another program, *Resumebest*, offers some of the same features as commercial resume preparation programs. It gives you various resume formats. The program tells you what to fill in for each section on your resume and also gives information concerning the proper order of presentation, the correct wording, and even what type of paper you should use (25-pound bond, plain white).

The Macintosh computer family offers *Personal Resume Writer*, which takes advantage of the Macintosh's graphics superiority to create a near-typeset-quality resume. You can play around with various fonts and customize the resume to your specifications. A Macintosh program called *Professional Resumewriter* uses templates to cut down on effort, time, and cost in resume preparation. The Apple family of computers provides a plethora of career preparation titles, but most cost hundreds of dollars and are designed for junior and senior high schools—as this is the leading computer used in educational settings.

Once you get that job, a program called *The Art of Negotiation* for the IBM/Compatible computer will propel you straight to the top. This software package takes advantage of the computer's ability to view a problem from many angles. If you know what you want but aren't sure how to get it, *The Art of Negotiation* may be what you need. The package comes with a book, *Fundamentals of Negotiating*, as well as a 500-page *Negotiation Manual* and a videotape by the author, who the documentation calls "The Father of Contemporary Negotiation." By the way, the ability to negotiate for what you want is one that can carry through in many areas of life, not just on the job. Just imagine yourself blowing them all away at the next garage sale you encounter!

LOVE AND RELATIONSHIP
SKILL-BUILDING SOFTWARE

Typical of the Love and Relationship genre of software is *Interaction* for the IBM/Compatible family of computers. Billed as an "educational entertainment device," *Interaction* lets you investigate unexplored features of your own and others' sex lives. The documentation for this provocative program claims that findings from over 100 sources were used to develop the questions—and pretty spicy questions they are, too. Based on scientific research, the questions lead from specific sexual behaviors to more general factors like personality and compatibility. (You can tell this is a piece of computer software because a question on whether you prefer computers to the opposite sex is not included. It can probably tell just by the touch of your fingers on the keyboard.)

Depending on your answer to the questions asked by this type of program, branching logic leads the program to ask you another, related question. These responses slowly add up to a personalized sexual analysis.

What's the benefit to this type of program? Besides the obvious entertainment value (you should have seen how the questions were greeted with shrieks and protests at a recent computer symposium), if you give candid answers you might learn something about yourself. And one of the programs, *The Love Quest*, offers users a complimentary registration in *The Love Quest* National Data Bank. The data bank will send you three names of people with similar answers to yours, free of charge. Like a computer dating service, the program charges a fee for every additional name forwarded after the first three.

Lets say you've met your dream mate after a spell in the National Data Bank, and now you're making wedding plans. A program for the Macintosh and IBM/Compatible computers can make sure the event is a smash hit. The program contains a checklist that covers dress fitting, buying the ring, renting tuxedos and arranging for a church. Scary, huh?

Things aren't going so well, and it's time for a few *Heart to Heart* talk sessions. This program encourages feuding couples to calm down and talk things over.

If you're just coming out of an unsuccessful relationship (one formed before you knew about love and relationship software), you need a good listener. After all, everyone on the job is sick of hearing about your lost love, and friends are starting to ignore your phone calls. It's time to turn to *Eliza*.

Created at MIT in 1966, *Eliza* is one of the world's most celebrated artificial intelligence demonstration programs. Her fame is due to the fact that she was able to convince people that they were actually conversing with an intelligent being (unlike some of the more unconvincing people you meet at parties). This program is able to act as a non-directive psychotherapist (one who just sits across the room from you and says "yes, go on . . ."). As you type in a statement, the program responds with its own comments or questions, which usually are a subtle twist on what you just told it. (Ahh, shrinks!)

The program can sometimes prove helpful when you just need to get something off your chest. *Eliza* comes with the source code, so lovelorn programmers can customize *Eliza*'s responses with a minimum of fuss.

If even your computer can't help you out in the ways of love, a shareware program for the IBM/Compatible family of computers might be able to at least terminate the relationship gracefully. *Divorce: Animated Strategy for Men* will educate you men out there on your rights and procedures (in California) to follow in case things just don't work out. The humorous program presents a series of graphic screens along with text concerning the legal matters of divorce. The documentation warns that "since it was written by a man for other men, [the program] does have a slight bias against women and marriage in general." Hmmmpf. And where's the women's edition?

CREATIVITY SOFTWARE

Are you tired of looking at a problem in the same old ways? Creativity enhancing software programs might be able to help you take a step back. Typical of this type of program is *The Idea Generator* for the IBM/Compatible family of computers. These programs enable fresh insights by making you isolate the problem and surround it with new concepts, generated by the computer's questions. *The Idea Generator* can be used in a group brainstorming session, because its report printing function helps everyone remember the meeting's objectives and outcome.

One of the best aids to imaginative thinking I've seen is a flaky-sounding shareware program called *Wisdom of the Ages*. The program asks you to go into dynamic mode. At the press of your return key, the program lists ten or so concepts, such as "failure," "travel," or "freedom," out of about a hundred. By highlighting the concept that interests you, a series of quotes comes on screen dealing with your chosen concept. After the "essential" category of quotations (in chronological order) is taken care of, you get categories like "opposites," "flowers" (poems, songs, and the like about your concept) and several other filters through which to view the concept you've chosen.

You can choose a concept directly from a menu, instead of letting the program choose them randomly. This would be a great resource for a writer, or for someone chatting on a Bulletin Board System who wants to have the perfect response to some philosophical discussion. Seeing how the sages have considered various ideas can spur some novel ways of looking at things for you.

HANDWRITING ANALYSIS ON DISK

Supposedly, the way you sign your name shows how you want to be seen by the world, while the way you write everything else shows the way you really are. Now you can explore the fascinating art of handwriting analysis via your versatile home computer.

A shareware program called, curiously enough, *Handwriting Analyst*, asks you several questions about a person's signature and then produces a summary on that person based on your responses.

In the report you get information on physical and material drives, intellectual style, personality traits, social behavior, and vocational implications. You can display on-screen, print, or write the report to a disk file. *Handwriting Analyst* lets you save the files for up to 20 signatures.

Some of *Handwriting Analyst*'s answers may be a little too close for comfort!

A commercial program for the Macintosh goes by the same name and offers most of the same features, as well.

ASTROLOGY SOFTWARE

Astrology programs really show off the power of the computer. If you're into astrology, your computer's calculating abilities are a vast improvement over the old way of figuring various angles, houses, and planetary positions (by hand, with a huge table of charts and houses).

If astrology is less a hobby and more a source of laughs to you, astrology software can quickly print out friends'charts—complete with short character descriptions. Numerous astrology programs abound for every type of computer operating system.

Two publishers put out dozens of programs apiece for the Macintosh family of computers. Astrolabe, Inc. and Time Cycles Research should be contacted by mail for a catalogue if you're at all interested in astrology. Astrolabe puts out the same titles for IBM/Compatibles.

The people at Zephyr put out *Horoscopics II*, which will print charts in column form or in wheel graphics form. A shareware program called *Astrol95* lets a person's future star positions (transits) be calculated for up to one year. The charts generated by this program can be saved to disk, reviewed, deleted, sorted alphabetically, and compared with other charts.

BIORHYTHM PROGRAMS

Are there times in the day when you're not feeling like yourself (or like anyone else, for that matter)? Perhaps your body just naturally slows down at these times. That's what the study of biorhythm is all about. Based on your birthdate, computer biorhythm programs can calculate what the condition of your emotional, physical, and intellectual capacities will be.

I-CHING, NUMEROLOGY, AND OTHER SOFTWARE

So many fun, bizarre fortune-telling software packages exist for every possible computer operating system. *Oracle-East* is a modern implementation of the ancient Chinese way of fortune telling, based on the 4000-year-old book, *I Ching*, or Book of Changes. It's been used by desperate souls longing to seek their future since before the time of Confucius. Tossing coins or picking arrow sticks was the traditional method of obtaining a trigram, two of which form the hexagrams from which I Ching readings are taken. Nature and a dualistic philosophy prevail in the teachings of this ancient source of wisdom.

Numerology is the "science" of assigning numerical values to concepts and items like names. Computers are great with numbers, so why not let your computer calculate everything around you and determine whether you're in sync with the universe? Some people take numerology so seriously they'll change their names if they don't add up right. Some folks name their computers; now your computer can name you!

Tarot cards can be a lot of fun, and the graphics capabilities of the Macintosh family of computers is a perfect way to show off the cards' neat designs. *Tarot Pack* is a *HyperCard* stack containing the complete Tarot deck. Another program for the Macintosh, called *Gypsy*, tells your fortune in several ways—and your wallet is still in your pocket when you quit the session.

SOURCES FOR PERSONAL GROWTH SOFTWARE

- *The Resume Kit*, $39.95 (IBM/Compatibles)
  Spinnaker Software Corp., One Kendall Square
  Cambridge, MA 02139, (617) 494-1200, (800) 826-0706

- *Apply* (Disk #1005)
  Resumebest (Disk #1097)
  (IBM/Compatibles)
  PC-SIG, 1030 East Duane Avenue, Ste. D
  Sunnyvale, CA 94086, (800) 222-2996 (CA)
  (800) 245-6717 (USA), (408) 730-9291

- *Personal Resume Writer*, $30.00 (Macintosh)
  Kinkos Academic Courseware Exchange, 225 W. Stanely Ave., Ste. A
  P.O. Box 8000, Ventura, CA 93002-8000, (800) 235-6919

- *Professional Resumewriter*, $100.00 (Macintosh)
  Bootware Software Co., Inc., 28024 Dorothy Dr.
  Agoura Hills, CA 91301, (818) 706-3887

- *The Art of Negotiating*, $495.00 (IBM/Compatibles)
  Experience in Software, Inc., 2039 Shattuck Ave., Ste. 401
  Berkely CA 94704, (415) 644-0694, (800) 678-7008

Love and Relationship Skill Building Software

- *Interaction*-analysis module, $59.95
  Interaction-compatibility module, $49.95
  The Love Quest, $59.95 (Apple Computers, Amiga Computers
  Commodore 64/128, IBM/Compatibles)
  Intracorp, Inc., 14160 S.W. 139th Ct.
  Miami, FL 33186, (800) 468-7226

- *Wedding Planner*, $10.00 (Macintosh)
  Heizer Software, 1941 Oak Park Blvd., Ste. 30
  Pleasant Hill, CA 94523, (415) 943-7667

- *Heart to Heart*, $39.95 (IBM/Compatibles)
  Interactive Software, 496 La Guardia Pl., Ste. 215
  NY NY 10012, (718) 768-1427

- *Eliza*, $45.00 (Apple Computers, IBM/Compatibles)
  Artificial Intelligence Research Group, 921 N. La Jolla Ave.
  LA CA 90046, (213) 656-7368

- *Divorce* (Disk #886), (IBM/Compatibles)
  PC-SIG, 1030 East Duane Avenue, Ste. D
  Sunnyvale, CA 94086, (800) 222-2996 (CA)
  (800) 245-6717 (USA), (408) 730-9291

Creativity Software

- *Idea Generator Plus*, $195.00 (IBM/Compatibles)
  Experience in Software, Inc., 2039 Shattuck Ave., Ste. 401
  Berkely CA 94704, (415) 644-0694, (800) 678-7008

- *Wisdom of the Ages*, $3.95 per disk; 4 disks
  Pan World International, P.O. Box 714
  Campbell, CA 95009

Handwriting Analysis on Disk

- *Handwriting Analyst*, $6.00 (IBM/Compatibles)
  PC-SIG, 1030 East Duane Avenue, Ste. D
  Sunnyvale, CA 94086, (800) 245-6717 (CA)
  (800) 245-6717 (USA), (408) 730-9291

- *Handwriting Analyst*, $69.95 (Macintosh)
  Ciasa, 2017 Cedar St.
  Berkeley, CA 94709, (415) 644-2771

Astrology Software

- (Send for Catalog), (Macintosh)
  Time Cycles Research, 27 Dimmock Rd.
  Waterford, CT 06385, (203) 444-6641

- (Send for Catalog), (Macintosh)
  Astrolabe, Inc., P.O. Box 28, 45 S. Orleans Rd.
  Orleans, MA 02653, (800) 255-0510

- *Horoscopics II*, $39.95 (IBM/Compatibles)
  Zephyr Services, 1900 Murray Ave.
  Pittsburgh, PA 15217, (412) 422-6600

- *Astrol95* (Disk #966), (IBM/Compatibles)
  PC-SIG, 1030 East Duane Avenue, Ste. D
  Sunnyvale, CA 94086, (800) 222-2996 (CA)
  (800) 245-6717 (USA), (408) 730-9291

Biorhythm Programs

- *Bio*Data*, $39.95 (IBM/Compatibles)
  Zephyr Services, 1900 Murray Ave.
  Pittsburgh, PA 15217, (412) 422-6600

- *Biorhythm Calculator*, $5.00 (Macintosh)
  Heizer Software, 1941 Oak Park Blvd., Ste. 30
  Pleasant Hill, CA 94523, (415) 943-7667

I-Ching, Numerology, and Other Software

- *Oracle-East*, $24.95 (IBM/Compatibles)
  Zephyr Services, 1900 Murray Ave.
  Pittsburgh, PA 15217, (412) 422-6600

- *Numberscope*, $39.95 (IBM/Compatibles)
  Zephyr Services, 1900 Murray Ave.
  Pittsburgh, PA 15217, (412) 422-6600

- *Personal Numerology*, $39.95 (Macintosh)
  Astrolabe, Inc., P.O. Box 28, 45 S. Orleans Rd.
  Orleans, MA 02653, (800) 255-0510

- *Tarot Pack*, $25.00 (Macintosh)
  Heizer Software, 1941 Oak Park Blvd., Ste. 30
  Pleasant Hill, CA 94523, (415) 943-7667

PART FOUR

CHAPTER 8

The Learning Tool:
Educational Software

Someone once said, "Education is what remains after people forget everything they learned in school." But education doesn't necessarily begin with that fearful first walk through the playground, nor should it end with the last dying strains of "Pomp and Circumstance."

Sure, you've been meaning to take that Chinese class after work, but the phrase "continuing education" always summons up the horrors of hunting for a parking place before Night School, figuring out the complex University Extension registration process, or stooping low enough to reach the drinking fountains at Adult Education sites.

If you have a home computer, your worries are over. Lessons and tutorials abound, all in the convenience of your own computer room and for a fraction of an extension course's cost. Learning is a lifelong process. With the right software, your computer can guide and inspire you in that process.

Remember, any experience can be viewed as educational under the right circumstances. Learning can take place even with "non-educational" software like games. The most important thing is to use your imagination. View each new software package you come across as a possible learning resource. Some of the most interesting packages I've encountered defy categorization, yet are educational nonetheless.

TASKS FOR EDUCATIONAL SOFTWARE

- Learning history
- Brushing up on domestic/international etiquette
- Familiarizing yourself with foreign cities/cultures
- Learning a foreign language
- Memorizing the constellations
- Learning the Bible
- Increasing typing speed
- Improving reading, math, and writing skills

History Software

Whether you choose to call *Footprints in History* a game, database, or educational program, this unique software package promotes learning history. It encourages family togetherness, too. When an individual's, or family's, personal events are entered into its historical database, *Footprints in History* generates a personalized time line, placing the personal event in the context of world history. You could sit Aunt Mary down at the next family reunion, quiz her on important milestones in her life such as high school graduation, engagement to Uncle Carl, etc., enter her data in her own VIP file on disk, and run off an archive combining her own events with those of the world.

Imagine how thrilled she'd be to see Gandhi's 200-mile march protesting salt tax in India, March 11, 1930—right next to the entry showing the day Cousin Elmo was born! And the whole family could gather round the printout and play "Remember when?," making Aunt Mary's time line the hit of the reunion. *Footprints in History* can be that perfect party or reunion ice-breaker, sparking hours of rewarding discussions and trips down memory lane for the entire family.

Time lines can be generated for a business or club as well as for individuals and families. And there are several categories of historical events from which to choose: international events, U.S. history, strange events, arts and entertainment, business, technology, and sports. Imagine generating a "Great Events in Technology" time line for a budding computer nerd, starting with his or her birthday and ending with a prize-winning science fair entry!

That Singular Day

If a time line spanning 1850 to the present is too much, *Footprints in History*'s publishers have put out a sister program, *Special Days*, that can spotlight memorable days for friends or family members.

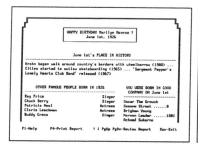
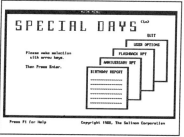

Figure 13: Single out that special day for a loved one.

Using *Special Days* is easy. Just insert the personal data (person's name, birthdate, anniversary date) into the program, and seconds later a display of trivia relating to that date appears on screen. Push a single key and an impressive printout is generated—complete with line-borders if your printer supports them. Kids and adults alike will marvel to find out what else was happening the day Grandpa was born, Mom and Dad married, or Sis won the Nobel Laureate. With a supply of parchment computer paper, thoughtful gifts suitable for framing can be created quickly.

Footprints in History and *Special Days* engage as educational tools because they blend personal history with "official" history—the best way to learn.

TRAVEL AND ETIQUETTE SOFTWARE

Software doesn't have to dwell in the past in order to be educational. With specialty software like *RSVP*, you can refine your knowledge of current mores and manners in the privacy of your own computer room. *RVSP* asks you to navigate your way through key social and business situations—and if you pick up the wrong fork, no one but your keyboard need know.

Miss Manners On-Line

RSVP lets you mind your Ps and Qs in two modes: game mode, or straight drill and practice. If you choose game mode, you're then asked to select a career. The first four career choices unfold in a domestic setting, while the last four let you make a fool out of yourself in countries all over the world. Depending on how you call each etiquette situation, you either rise meteorically in your chosen career or fail dismally, destined to a life of slurping soup with your dessert spoon.

The game mode offers one tiny catch: you need a good memory. From time to time an appointment book or note message flashes on screen, when you're informed of such facts as Mr. Smith hates cats but loves dogs. Consider yourself warned when you blow it and drag Fluffy along to that networking breakfast!

The drill mode is an effective way to hammer down the manners of a particular country before a trip—whether for business or pleasure. Selecting national situations displays a menu of 17 categories ranging from Telephone Manners to Men and Women to Weekends Out. And for those with dinner napkin tucked firmly under chin, never fear—the Table Manners category is followed closely by the More Table Manners category.

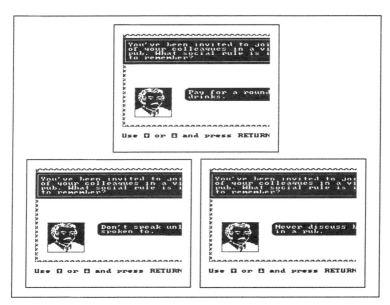

Figure 14: *Learn how to handle yourself when drinking in Australia, with* RVSP.

RVSP helps you keep in mind the basic tenet of manners—consideration for others—and does so with a sense of humor. While polishing their veneers, players will learn the fascinating customs and quirks of 19 foreign nations. Now, in which country was it a must to show enjoyment of a meal by burping . . . ?

Traveling Light

Now you've got those weird customs down, thanks to *RSVP*. But if you really want to familiarize yourself with a particular country, a new breed of travel simulation software can help you learn more about that nation's art, geography, food, wine, banking, transportation, shopping, and even a bit of the language.

Ticket to Paris, and its sister programs *Ticket to London*, *Ticket to Spain*, and *Ticket to Washington, D.C.* (what language do you learn for that one?) challenge you to learn your way around and overcome various travel situations while solving a puzzle.

Ticket to Paris's scenario unfolds as follows: Your family has begged you to travel to Paris and track down an errant cousin who refuses to come back home. Unless you bone up on French life and culture, your chances for finding the roving relative are slim. The program has you holding conversations and answering questions, using money wisely, visiting restaurants and museums, and being rewarded for your new experiences with clues. Don't forget to pay your hotel bill! (How come *my* family never sends me on such missions?)

One aspect of *Ticket to Paris* seems ridiculous. A rather moronic hunger-and-fatigue module requires you to pay attention to your physical well-being by resting enough and remembering to consume at least 24 nutritional points per day. The time clock ticks away relentlessly, and if you forget to eat, you end up in the hospital.

Now, I ask you, who could forget to eat in *Paris*?

Another drawback is the constant barrage of questions greeting you at every hotel lobby or bistro. The questions are rarely in context, they're difficult, and you only get two tries. Since scoring points (and finding your cousin) depends on correctly answering the pesky woman relentlessly firing questions at you out of the blue, it would have been nice if the software program included a booklet or text file discussing question topics in the context of French history, geography, and culture. I missed many of the more obscure questions; having traveled to France a few times, lived there one summer, and minored in French in college, I can only imagine the frustration this game would hold for someone preparing to go over there for the first time.

These are minor drawbacks in an otherwise excellent package. Those who are eagerly preparing for a trip abroad, as well as those who are eagerly staying home for some rest and relaxation, will enjoy this version of armchair (computer chair?) travel.

FOREIGN LANGUAGE PROGRAMS

Loaded with the right foreign language software, your computer will compare only to your seventh-grade Spanish teacher in its steadfast determination to drill a new language into your brain.

If you haven't yet studied a foreign language, computer software can be a firm, yet patient, teacher. And if you just need a little practice for that upcoming trip, dozens of language programs can show you how to ask where the bathroom is with finesse.

Hola, Bonjour, Guden Tag

Combining the best features of databases and word processors, a good language program can conjugate any verb, give noun forms and genders, give tips on style and usage, and even search and replace from English into the acquired language.

One series of programs, MicroTac's *Language Assistant* software programs, even offers an accent-entry feature, where you just hit a hot-key combination (Control-'), the letter you want accented, and the accent mark. Voila, a freshly accented character pops up right in the middle of your word processor document.

Most language programs come with complete verb conjugations. Having every verb tense, form, and person available at the touch of a key is something I would have killed for in college. (Then again, a computer would have been handy in college, too.) The Macintosh desk accessory *Le conjugueur*'s sole purpose in life is to supply the correct conjugation of all the French verbs.

Designed for those who use French often in their work or study, this program is a must. The *Assistant* programs mentioned above supply a complete explanation of each verb tense's use, at the touch of a function key. Now you can finally discover the purpose of those 50 Spanish subjunctive tenses.

Bilingual dictionaries are almost always included in full-featured language programs. By typing in either the English or target-language word in the *Assistant* programs, the translation pops up on the screen.

Synonyms are no problem. For the English word "slip," for example, you get the foreign translation for the woman's undergarment and the verb "to slip." The memory-resident mode lets you hit the enter key from within your word processor and the translation sticks itself right into your document. Another program, *SpanGlish*, a Macintosh Spanish/English spelling dictionary, contains over 40,000 of the most commonly misspelled words from both languages. These programs recognize that language is a changing process, so you can add words and alter definitions to your liking.

On the public domain front, *Language Teacher* is a series of menu-driven language tutorial programs designed to be run on the IBM PC/XT/AT/jr or any compatible clone. Each program in the series contains hundreds of word combinations and verb conjugation forms.

The program lets you select language-to-English or English-to-language combinations, multiple-choice answers, be retested on misses, print a multiple-choice test, and run a full quiz diagnostic routine with line printer output. Of particular interest to non-English students is the option to select the direction of the combinations.

All word, phrase, and verb conjugation selections are randomly generated by the program, so the user is unable to predict the next selection. The program package is not designed to teach conversational language or pronunciation but, instead, to provide practice drills in order to increase your working vocabulary and to enhance your use of the conjugation forms.

I tried out the "Spanish I" module, and although the vocabulary words were easy, I found myself trying to outrace the time clock and enjoying every minute. Good practice, especially for the program's price: free.

The shareware program *Japanese Tutor* can help widen your Eastern horizons. The program is menu-driven. It teaches beginning Japanese vocabulary and grammar. Designed for students and travelers alike, it's a good value. Another Asian language shareware disk is *Cantonese Tutor*. This menu-driven program is designed to be combined with classroom instruction, as Chinese needs to be heard. Customizing lessons is possible.

War of the Words

Combining fun and learning is what computers are all about. A program called *Battle of Words* lets you test your translation skills in the atmosphere of a fast-paced arcade game. After a series of word definitions and sample sentences, the program quizzes you. Finally, you face a colorful arcade game where you try to find the correct translations as quickly as possible. The graphics and sound help to hold your interest. A neat feature is the ability to create your own vocabulary lists, exercises and tests.

Where Were You on the Night of the . . .

Another foreign language program that makes learning fun is *Whodunit* for the Mac. You can solve a mystery in either French, German, or Spanish, by choosing the right answers when the program asks you questions. (Don't worry; the butler did it.)

ASTRONOMY SOFTWARE

Foreign language software can help you travel the world, but wouldn't it be nice to be able to travel to other worlds? You can, merely by loading an astronomy software package into your home computer. Think of how prepared you'll be when Earth is overtaken by interplanetary aliens.

Most astronomy programs are based on celestial databases. Generally you can focus in on various galactic phenomena, or check out the sky for any given date. One astronomy program, *Voyager* for the Macintosh, really shines.

At the heart of the *Voyager* astronomy program is its 14,000-object database, including 9,100 stars, 3,000 deep-space objects (galaxies, etc.), 88 constellation outlines, the planets in our solar system, and more. Not only can you view the night sky from anywhere on earth (specifying either one of 135 earthly cities, or any longitude and latitude) but from any planet too. You can even get really weird and view the sky from deep space. The sky can be viewed as a star chart and a celestial sphere as well.

You get to select your point of view from time, as well as from space. *Voyager* can display the heavens on any date from 1000 B.C. to A.D. 4000. If any planet, star, or nebula sparks further interest, you can click on it and up pops a data box. The box tells you more about its name, Yale number, type, distance, magnitude, location coordinates—everything you ever wanted to know about that celestial object but were afraid to ask.

Software publisher Zephyr Services offers a whole range of astronomy programs. Space allows mention of only a few; if you're a dedicated astronomer, you should write away for their catalogue.

Astrofinder offers skyviews for your date, time, and location, and lets you filter out lesser star magnitudes to make the display easier to see. With a deep-sky object file, you can add and delete comets, planets and other space objects. Zephyr's *Suntracker* calculates astronomical conditions for any solar eclipse and displays a map with areas of visibility. The program computes and provides eclipse elements, accurate to 12 miles on the Earth's surface. You can input your own elements to achieve greater accuracy as well.

Moontracker does the same thing but for lunar eclipses. *Cometwatch* teaches all about comets, how and when to observe them, and even how to photograph them. *Astrocalc* features all the basic astronomical data for any date and location.

Have you ever gone out to the desert, looked up at the night sky, and wished you knew the names of all those stars? Zephyr's *Astrostell* teaches the various constellations, their lore, and the stars that comprise them. You can see the more common star formations, have the program pick constellations at random and quiz you for their names, or select among the 88 specific constellations listed. The program also offers hints on how to get started stargazing, and teaches the history of constellation discovery as well as the history of star mapping.

BIBLE SOFTWARE

Gazing at the heavens through your computer screen may inspire you to ponder the heavens through your computer screen. What better means to finding out the meaning of it all than loading your computer with Bible software? Even if your beliefs lie outside the Judeo/Christian tradition, the Bible is a valuable source of wisdom, inspiration, and just plain good reading.

What's the advantage to having the Bible on your computer? Bible software typically offers the entire Bible in the form of a database, making it easy to search for a particular word or combination of words. You can also search for specific sections or verses. Listings of all that word's or phrase's appearances come up instantaneously. This makes it easy to trace an idea or theme throughout the Bible.

The Bible program *WORDsearch*, for the MS-DOS family, is especially helpful for people who may use a computer as a tool, but not as a hobby in itself. The on-screen help menus and manual are written in a non-threatening, step-by-step style. The program is capable of searching the entire Bible for a word in two seconds. Another plus is the note feature, where you can record your thoughts and studies, combine them with other notes and verses, and print them out—a real benefit to clergy or others who work regularly with the Bible.

A Macintosh program called *MacBible* takes advantage of the Mac's superior graphics capabilities by offering Bible graphics, maps, and charts, as well as a 25-disk volume of the King James Bible with chapter and verse search.

It's easy to bone up on Bible facts and figures with a shareware program for the PC/compatible family called *Bible Quiz Plus*. The program is billed as a religious trivia game with three different levels of play. One to six seekers can play. Questions can be answered in multiple choice, fill-in-the-blank, or answer-only mode. Printable, the questions are from the Books of Psalms and Proverbs.

A user option lets you create your own questions. *Bible Quiz Plus* is fun to play and is a great educational tool for children and adults alike.

Another Bible program, *Scripture Bits* for the Macintosh family of computers, lets you generate a verse for every day in the year. A Topics feature lets you search for specific subjects from "Acceptance" to "Youth," arranged alphabetically. A Quotations section holds pearls of wisdom taken from the book of Acts to Zephaniah, and a Religious Charts section holds Old and New Testament chronology charts. The program is available in either English or Spanish as well. Buy the Spanish version and learn two things at once: wisdom from the Bible and a foreign language.

Those who find themselves writing often about the Bible may find the Macintosh software program *Bible Spelling Dictionary* handy. This program features a 20,000-word religious dictionary that contains all of the unique words, names, places, abbreviations and topics of the Old and New Testaments, including the obsolete spellings in the King James version of the Bible. Customizing the dictionary is easy to do in case a new archeological find in the Holy Land is uncovered by bomb blasts.

TYPING TUTORS

Just about every computer-adept person I've met is able to type extremely rapidly. I'm not sure which came first, the fast typing ability or the computer ability, but this can't be mere coincidence. So, learn to type even faster and start down the road to Computer Guru-dom today.

With one of the many good typing tutor software packages out there, your computer can assess your skill level, drill you on problem areas, and even let you customize your own lessons, in the case of *Mavis Beacon Teaches Typing!*, for the IBM/Compatible family of computers.

The true advantage of computer typing tutors is their ability to automatically adjust to a user's abilities. Compare this with the old method of taking the page out of the typewriter, then circling all the mistakes you made, charting all the letters mistyped, and then turning to each of the drills focusing on those letters.

Most typing programs feature some sort of metronome or clock ticking in order to give you a sense of rhythm while pounding away on the keyboard. It's easy to disable this feature if it drives you nuts. You can turn off and on the "guide hands" option in many programs too. *Mavis Beacon* lets you save your setup preferences for next time you use the program.

Positive feedback is important in a learning situation, and most programs display a graph or chart of your progress. *Mavis Beacon* lets you print a report card too. (But you don't get a chocolate coin when you do extra well, as in Madame Rigsby's sophomore French class.)

Mavis Beacon Teaches Typing! is *almost* "the finest typing program in the world," as its box proclaims. Alas, the program is copy-protected, and demands that you insert the "key" disk on and off throughout your session with the program. What a hassle.

The ability to print results gives you a personal record of the speed/accuracy goals you set. You can monitor whether or not you're actually making progress. *Typing Tutor IV* for the Macintosh has you complete a goals questionnaire that asks you about your current level of experience and desired typing speed.

On the shareware front, the *Touchtype* disk from PC-SIG (#320) for IBM/Compatibles is a complete program that ranges from beginning to advanced skill levels. With CGA-quality graphics and configurable features, this program has almost as much going for it as commercial IBM/Compatible programs—at a fraction of the cost.

READIN', WRITIN', 'RITHMETIC

Computers aren't just good for learning esoteric stuff like international etiquette or Cantonese Chinese. Once in a while it's good to brush up on the basics, and reading, writing, and arithmetic software is a good place to start. Several programs exist in each of these categories for every operating system imaginable.

College Entrance Exam Preparation Programs

Using your home computer during the course of your college career is smart. But you can start taking advantage of the computer's educational capabilities long before you're accepted to a college or university. Scholastic Aptitude Test (SAT) preparation software programs exist for every type of computer operating system. The programs are similar to each other. They all contain tests for each of the SAT's sections: Verbal, Math, and Logic.

The Perfect Score: Computer Preparation for the SAT for the Macintosh series of computers comes with a bonus program: a college selection database called *The Perfect College*. Barron's, the publishers of the familiar softcover college prep workbooks, offers an IBM/Compatible preparation program with modules that analyze the student's answers and pinpoint weaknesses and strengths.

Barron's Computer Study Program for the SAT offers tests in two modes: Testing Mode, which simulates real test conditions, and Learning Mode. Learning Mode gives you *two* chances to answer those typical SAT questions, like: If five people each wore yellow overalls except Mary, and the two named Fred lost red galoshes last Thursday, but the bus only stops at Fourth and Main at 2 p.m. every other Tuesday, what day will Easter fall on this year?

Speed Reading Programs

Whether you're trying to get into the college of your choice, or just trying to read all the trade journals and other materials that pile up at work every week, speed reading is a great skill to acquire. The computer is ideally suited to reading instruction because words can flash across an otherwise blank screen and successfully hold your attention like no book can.

Flashread, a speed reading program for the IBM/Compatibles, forces the eye to focus on three words at a time. Since the eye can transmit information to the brain only when it isn't moving, reading one word at a time results in jumpy eye movements that slow the flow of information to the brain. Practice with *Flashread* can increase your peripheral vision, allowing you to read larger word groupings.

After a diagnostic test to determine your reading index number, the program enters the "linear reading" mode, where groups of three words flash across the screen at your optimum reading speed level. Your eyes are forced to fixate on the groups of words—and you begin to automatically read at your most efficient rate. When you're reading effortlessly and most efficiently, *Flashread* calls this the fusion level.

Once you hit fusion level, the linear reading mode subtly speeds up. I wanted to slow it down a tad by hitting the space bar (which you can do any time during practice), but after deciding against changing my reading index number, I reentered practice mode again to find it had slowed by itself. Good. I was getting dizzy.

Two programs for the Macintosh contain eye exercises designed to strengthen eye muscles as well as improve eye-movement rates. *Speed Reading Tutor IV* puts you through your paces in a rousing session of "Eyeobics," while *Speed Reader II* contains six muscle building activities.

Reading and Reasoning

Queue publishes the *Lessons in Reading and Reasoning I - IV* series for all the computer families. These programs teach you how to spot fallacies in what you read. You can become a more critical reader (and thinker).

Building Writing Skills

Computers may make writing easier, but what if you could use your computer to make your writing better? Many style and grammar checker programs exist. The better ones offer tips to improve your choice of words and sentence length.

Readability for IBM/Compatible computers is one of the best writing aids around. Save an example of your writing as a text file, and bring it into *Readability*. Choose one of nine categories of writing you think it fits. Categories range from "Children's books" to "Magazine feature articles" to "Bureaucratic gobbledygook." You can see at a glance how your writing measures up in any of 16 diagrams. Suggestions to increase your writing's readability follow. The hardcover manual is extensive and well-researched.

Math Programs

As with so many types of educational software, math programs number in the thousands. One of the most versatile shareware programs for the IBM/Compatible computers is *Math Pak II*, which can bring you up to speed in everything from very basic arithmetic to calculus, trigonometry, and geometry.

Plusses and Minuses

As far as the foreign language programs go, one of the *Language Assistant* series' drawbacks is that the screen colors are not configurable. Because of incompatibility with my word processor's screen (*WordPerfect*), I had to suffer through orange text on a red background while in the memory-resident mode. Not very easy to see. The stand-alone display looked just fine.

Also, don't rely on the *Language Assistant* series' "Replace Word for Word" feature for anything other than the most basic guidelines to foreign word order, grammar, and vocabulary. Although the manual does warn that you're to use "your skills and the Assistant to refine the document" afterwards—don't bother unless that foreign language is really Greek to you. This feature was made for that panic-ridden cram night when a 10-page translation is due and you haven't cracked a book all semester. Only a desperate person would consider using it. It's *that* rough.

In matters celestial, *Astrostell* will happily list all the constellations you can see at any one time, date, and locale, but after displaying your first choice, it bounces back into the main menu and you have to start all over again by entering—you guessed it—date, time and locale. You should be able to preview, and print out if you wish, all the constellations visible that night. One way to get around this is to print the screen which lists the visible star formations for that date, and then go to the main constellation menu and select the various constellations by number.

EDUCATIONAL SOFTWARE

History

- *Footprints in History,* $39.95
  Special Day, $39.95 (IBM/Compatibles)
  The Salinon Corporation, P.O. Box 31047
  Dallas, TX 75231, (800) 722-0054, (214) 692-9091

Etiquette

- *RSVP*, $39.95, *Ticket to . . .* series
  (Apple II series, Commodore 64/128,
  IBM/Compatibles, Macintosh)
  Blue Lion Software, 90 Sherman Street
  Cambridge, MA 02140, (617) 876-2500, (800) 333-0199

Foreign Language

- *The Language Assistant Series*, $49.95 ea. (IBM/Compatibles)
  Spanish, French, German, Italian
  MicroTac Software, 4655 Cass St., Ste. 304
  San Diego, CA 92109, (619) 272-5700

- *Le conjuguer*, $49.95 (Macintosh)
  Les editions Ad Lib, Inc., 220 Grande Allee est, Ste. 960
  Quebec, Canada G1R 2J1, (418) 529-9676, (800) 463-2686

- *SpanGlish*, $32.95 (Macintosh)
  Medina Software, Inc., 2008 Las Palmas Cir.
  Orlando, FL 32822, (305) 281-1557

- *Language Teacher* , free (IBM/Compatibles)
  Spanish, French, German, Italian
  Micro Tutor Products, 103 Baughmans Lane, Ste. 303
  Frederick, MD 21701
  or
  PC-SIG, 1030 East Duane Avenue, Ste. D
  Sunnyvale, CA 94086, (800) 222-2996 (CA)
  (800) 245-6717 (USA), (408) 730-9291

- *Japanese Tutor* (Disk #712)
  Cantonese Tutor (Disk #755)
  (IBM/Compatibles)
  PC-SIG, 1030 East Duane Avenue, Ste. D
  Sunnyvale, CA 94086, (800) 222-2996 (CA)
  (800) 245-6717 (USA), (408) 730-9291

- *Battle of Words*, $49.95 (IBM/Compatibles)
  Gessler Publishing Co., 55 W. 13th St.
  NY NY 10011, (212) 627-0099

- *Whodunit*, $49.95 (Macintosh) 512K and up
  Gessler Educational software, 900 Broadway
  New York, NY 10003, (212) 673-3113

Astronomy Programs

- *Voyager*, $99.50 (Macintosh)
  Carina Software, 830 Williams St.
  San Leandro, CA 94577, (415) 352-7328

- *AstroFinder*, $69.95 (IBM/Compatibles) *Suntracker*, $29.95
  (IBM/Compatibles, Apple II family, Commodore 64/128)
  Astrocalc, $29.95
  (IBM/Compatibles, Apple II family, Commodore 64/128)
  Moontracker, $29.95
  (IBM/Compatibles, Apple II family, Commodore 64/128)
  Astrostell, $29.95 (IBM/Compatibles, Apple II family)
  Cometwatch, $29.95
  (IBM/Compatibles, Apple II family, Commodore 64/128)
  Zephyr Services, 1900 Murray Avenue
  Pittsburgh, PA 15217, (412) 422-6600, (800) 533-6666

Bible Software

- *WORDsearch*, $9.00 (IBM/Compatibles) Hard disk required
  WORDworks Software Architects, 5014 Lakeview Drive
  Austin, TX 78732, (512) 266-9898, (800) 888-9898

- *MacBible*, $129.00, *MacBible Concordance*, $75.00
  (Macintosh) Hard disk required
  Encycloware, 712 Washington St.
  Ayden, NC 28513, (919) 746-4961

- *MacConcord I*, $42.95, *MacGospel* , $24.95, *MacScripture*, $119.95,
  Scripture Bits, $22.00, *Bible Spelling Dictionary*, $24.95
  (Macintosh) Hard disk required
  Medina Software, Inc., 2008 Las Palmas Cir.
  Orlando, FL 32822, (305) 281-1557

Typing Tutors

- *Mavis Beacon Teaches Typing*, $49.95 (IBM/Compatibles)
  The Software Toolworks, One Toolworks Plaza, 13557 Ventura Blvd.,
  Sherman Oaks, CA 91423, (818) 907-6789

- *Typing Tutor IV*, $49.95 (Macintosh)
  Simon & Schuster Software, 1 Gulf + Western Plaza, 14th Fl.
  NY, NY 10023, (213) 373-8882, (800) 624-0023

- *PC-Fastype* (Disk #320), (IBM/Compatibles)
  PC-SIG, 1030 East Duane Avenue, Ste. D
  Sunnyvale, CA 94086, (800) 222-2996 (CA)
  (800) 245-6717 (USA), (408) 730-9291

College Entrance Exam Preparation Software

- *The Perfect Score:*
  Computer Preparation for the SAT, $79.95 (Macintosh)
  Mindscape, Inc., 3444 Dundee Rd.
  Northbrook, IL 60062, (800) 221-9884

- *SAT Score Improvement System*, $99.95 (Macintosh)
  Spinnaker Software Corp., 1 Kendall Sq.
  Cambridge, MA 02139, (617) 494-1222

- *Barron's Computer Study Program for the SAT*, $49.95
  Barron's Computer Study Program for the ACT, $79.95
  (IBM/Compatibles)
  Barron Educational Series, 250 Wireless Blvd.
  Hauggauge, NY 11788, (516) 434-3311

Reading, Writing, and Arithmetic Programs

- *Flashread*, $49.95 (IBM/Compatibles)
  PVA Systems, 7777 Fay Ave., Ste. K
  La Jolla, CA 92037, (619) 456-0707

- *Speed Reading Tutor IV*, $49.95
  Simon & Shuster Software, 1 Gulf + Western Plaza, 14th Floor
  New York, NY 10023, (212) 373-8882, (800) 624-0023

- *Speed Reader II*, $69.95 (Macintosh)
  Davidson & Associates, Inc., 3135 Kashiwa St.
  Torrance, CA 90505, (213) 534-4070, (800) 556-6141

- *Lessons in Reading and Reasoning I - IV*, $49.95 ea.
  (All Types of Computers)
  Queue, 562 Boston Ave.
  Bridgeport, CA 06610-1705, (203) 335-0908

- *Readability*, $94.95 (IBM/Compatibles)
  Scandinavian PC Systems, Inc., 51 Monroe St., Ste. 707A
  Rockville, MA 20850, (301) 294-7450

- *Math Pak II* (Disk #394), (IBM/Compatibles)
  PC-SIG, 1030 East Duane Avenue, Ste. D
  Sunnyvale, CA 94086, (800) 222-2996 (CA)
  (800) 245-6717 (USA), (408) 730-9291

CHAPTER 9

Graphically Speaking

Squiggles. Circles. Lines. Colors. Ever since the era of cave paintings, humans have wanted to capture the world around them in graphic images. We've evolved from using hairy bison and giant antelopes as models, but the process of capturing reality in form, color, and line still fascinates us.

Long gone are those peaceful Paleolithic afternoons when anyone could simply trace a charred twig along a handy cave wall to achieve lasting arthood. Art supplies in the Space Age are messy, complex, and expensive. Fortunately, there's a solution to this dilemma. (No, get away from those walls with that charred Q-Tip!)

If you own a computer, a fully-equipped art studio can be at your disposal with paint programs. The precision tools of a graphic artist are yours with draw programs. Other graphics software programs offer printing press capabilities, so you can design stationery, banners, greeting cards—even business cards and letterhead for that home business you always wanted to start up. EGA and VGA graphics demo programs are fun to run and collect. Animation programs let you add pizazz to your computer programs and presentations. Special printer ribbons are even available—to enable transfer of your designs to T-shirts and other clothing. Computer graphics programs make it fun and easy to create art. The possiblilities are limited only by your imagination.

Unlike setting up a real art studio, your computer art studio needs very little in the way of supplies. If you have an IBM/Compatible, you will need some type of graphic adapter card. A Hercules Graphics Card (or one of its clones) will do the job with a monochrome monitor. Color monitors give you that artist feel. Depending on the color monitor you choose, you'll need a CGA, EGA, or VGA card to drive the monitor. A mouse or joystick is recommended; be sure to check the graphics software package to see if you must have one of these to be able to run the program.

USES FOR GRAPHICS SOFTWARE

- Illustrations, Posters, Charts, Doodling
- Animation
- Creating Cards, Stationery, Banners
- Viewing EGA/VGA Demos
- Slide Generation
- Enhancing Home Videos

PAINT PROGRAMS

With paint programs, you'll get an art studio for a lot less than you'd pay for brushes, gesso, an airbrush kit, paints, canvases, and more (unlike software, paints and brushes get used up).

Paint programs allow you to create art for presentations, newsletters, or just for art's sake. (Now it's *your* turn to hang art on the refrigerator.) Every paint program has basically the same approach as an artist working manually. First you select a tool from an opening menu. Tools can be brushes, erasers, airbrushes, or automatic lines, boxes, circles, and so on. Just as an artist would choose a fine brush for detail work, you can vary the width of the electronic brush or eraser from one to several pixels wide and vary the shape from square to round.

Color is selected from a strip displaying the entire rainbow. But an artist seldom uses a color straight out of the tube. Half the fun is mixing various blobs of paint on a palette—then tossing the muddy brown results. Palettes in paint programs are fun, too, allowing you to mix in new colors a pixel at a time until you end up with all these neat checkerboards on your screen.

Most paint programs offer the capability of altering the 16 colors displayed at any one time on an EGA monitor from the 64 available. The zoom feature is a standard with most of these programs as well, allowing you to perform delicate color shading pixel by pixel.

Other finishing touches can be performed with grids, move/copy features, reductions, smoothing, tilting, rotating, flipping, and a host of other features offered only on a computer. Choosing a pathname under which to save the masterpiece and printing it are the only steps left between you and fame.

Advantages and Disadvantages

Despite their many similarities, paint programs vary in their basic philosophies. The creators of *EGA Paint*, for example, believe that having to move the cursor over to a menu each time you want to change a tool or color breaks the artistic flow and wastes time. Thus their programs are based on pop-up menus that appear on screen with the touch of a key or the flick of a mouse. When you switch to menu mode during a drawing session, the current cursor position is frozen and a small menu window is displayed. Selection made, the cursor returns automatically to its last position.

This is a radical departure from the look and feel of most paint programs, *PC Paintbrush* included. The plus is that you get that "blank cave-wall" feel; a black screen is all you see at first. The minus is that you may have trouble remembering how to access a particular menu. Luckily, a flow chart is provided to ease the transition. An added bonus: *EGA Slide*, a slideshow presentation program, is included with *EGA Paint*. In comparison, *PC Paintbrush*'s presentation program, *PC Presentation*, costs another $95. The manuals for both programs are well written and presented; *PC Paintbrush*'s has a slight edge in that it illustrates features with friendly looking, amateur level graphics that feel homey.

DRAWING PROGRAMS

Object-oriented graphics programs, or "drawing" programs, let you manipulate basic shapes with much more flexibility than bit-mapped "paint" programs. The reason these types of programs are so appealing is that they bring computer graphics up to the level of CAD, or Computer Aided Design.

Draw programs' basic tools are circles, arcs, ellipses, lines, squares, curves, polygons, and other primitives that can be individually placed, combined, and sized anywhere on the page. However, if you have bit-mapped images from scanners or paint programs that you want to use, you can import them into draw programs and trace over them to get object-oriented maneuverability. These imported bit-mapped images can be stretched, colored, cropped, and zoomed, but not totally edited.

Plusses and Minuses

Any feature contained in a regular paint or draw program is refined to the highest degree in *Designer*, an IBM/Compatible draw program. Most graphics programs give you colors; *Designer* gives you 3.6 million (only your screen limits how many colors you can see). The working area of this program can get positively out of hand: up to 48 pages long and 8½ by 11 inches wide.

The list of super features is calculated to make a non-Mac user drool with greed. Rotating objects and text in 1/10 of a degree increments is easy. You can set line widths from 1/1000 of an inch to one inch. Up to 64 layers can be defined in your drawing, restricted to a certain color if you wish, and each layer can be named in plain English (for example, "muscles" or "skeletal"). However, *Designer* is priced a bit steeply for the average home user. And getting up to speed on this complex, powerful program can take some time.

Drawing Table offers a powerful feature that manages multiple documents in progress as a "project." You can leave right in the middle of creating several works, come back, and everything is just as you left it. This program also imports paint, PICT, and EPSF images.

Clip Art

Draw programs generally come with a clip art library. Samplings of the 400 general symbols included in one program consist of planes, animals, borders, computer components, flags, furniture, maps landmarks, familiar objects, signs of the zodiac, and space vehicles. Additional clip art disks are usually very reasonably priced.

These programs are aimed mostly at graphic artists, professional illustrators, architects, engineers, and desktop publishers. They are compatible with the software programs used every day in these professions. Drawing programs are popular with home-published writers/artists, since ASCII files and *Windows* Clipboard Text can be imported. Experimental artists, too, will love these programs.

SLIDE GENERATION

Have you ever wished you could immortalize graphics or other screens created on your computer? Many graphics programs can be used for the production of quality slides and overhead transparencies. One shareware program in particular, *Slide Generation*, is dedicated to this purpose. Images may be created, edited, saved, displayed and printed. Overhead transparencies are produced by copying the printed output onto transparent material. Photographic slides are made by photographing the printed output.

PRINTING PRESS PROGRAMS

Programs such as *Print Shop* and *Print Magic* let you make greeting cards, banners, letterhead, and more. The menu-driven programs are easy to use. Children will love the ability to select a graphic and have it automatically pasted into their documents.

ANIMATION PROGRAMS

Paint and draw progams give you great printouts, but what if you could find a way to embellish the screen you stare at daily? Or, you can turn your computer into a professional animation studio and create a dazzling presentation telling the kids to take out the garbage instead of verbally nagging them to do so.

Animation programs allow you to create your own movies, with fades, dissolves, even music and sound effects on a Macintosh computer. These programs are easy enough to figure out—just create one "track" at a time and blend them all together for a stunning effect.

EGA/VGA DEMOS

You loved that EGA demo at the dealer's, and, er, well, now you're the proud owner of the latest Lightning-Switch Monitor and Graphics Card. But how will you show off your new purchase? Let's face it, the average word processor or database menu just doesn't take full advantage of your monitor's resolution—or those great colors your EGA or VGA card provides.

Wouldn't it be nice to have some graphics demos handy for those times when people find out just how much you spent on that monitor and graphics card—and ask: "but what does it do?" Graphics demos are available from dealers or from electronic BBSs (Bulletin Board Systems). They're fun to collect and even more fun to watch.

WHERE TO BUY GRAPHICS PROGRAMS

Paint Programs

- *EGA Paint 2005* , $129.00 (IBM/Compatible)
  RIX SoftWorks, Inc., 18552 MacArthur Blvd., Ste. 375
  Irvine, CA 92715, (800) 233-5983 (CA), (800) 345-9059 (USA)

- *PC Paintbrush*, $95.00 (IBM/Compatible)
  ZSoft Corporation, 450 Franklin Road, Ste. 100
  Marietta, GA 30067, (404) 428-0008

Drawing Programs

- Micrografx *Designer*, $695.00 (IBM/Compatible)
  Micrografx, 1820 N. Greenville Ave.
  Richardson, TX 75081, (214) 234-1769

- *Drawing Table*, $129.95 (Mac Plus, SE, II)
  Broderbund Software, 17 Paul Dr.
  San Rafael, CA 94903-2101, (800) 527-6263, (415) 492-3500

- *PC-Key Draw*, $100.00 (IBM/Compatibe)
  PC-SIG, INC., 1030 E. Duane Ave., Ste. D
  Sunnyvale, CA 94086

Printing Press Programs

- *The Print Shop* (Apple II Series) $49.95, (Mac Plus, SE) $59.95
  (IBM/Compatible) $59.95 (Commodore Series) $44.95 (Atari) $44.95
  Broderbund Software, 17 Paul Dr.
  San Rafael, CA 94903-2101, (800) 521-6263, (415) 492-3500

Slide Generation Programs

- *Slide Generation*, $25.00 (IBM/Compatible)
  PC-SIG, INC., 1030 E. Duane Ave., Ste. D
  Sunnyvale, CA 94086

Animation Programs

- *VideoWorks II*, $195.00 (Mac 512, Plus, SE)
  Broderbund Software, 17 Paul Dr.
  San Rafael, CA 94903-2101, (800) 527-6263, (415) 492-3500

- *TheDraw*, $15.00 (IBM/Compatible)
  TheSoft Programming Services, 1929 Whitecliff Court
  Walnut Creek, CA 94596

CHAPTER 10

The Computer at Large: Telecommunications

A modem is the least computer-like thing you can buy for your computer. Now, it's true that modems and computers have a few things in common. Modems, like computers, quickly perform routine or repetitive tasks. For example, modems can redial phone numbers in a flash. And modems are able to record keystrokes and play them back later, just like computer programs with macro capabilities. But buying a modem and going on-line lets you meet and communicate with people—something most computer applications don't offer at all.

Once you've equipped your computer with a modem and some communications software, your computer can call local and national BBSs, or Bulletin Board Systems. Hobbyists just like you and me have set up computers in their own homes and equipped them with modems and bulletin board software so that other people with modems can call and leave messages (just like a "real" bulletin board), play games, discuss issues, download software— the possibilities are endless. Zillions of Bulletin Board Systems are waiting for you to call. Each has its distinct personality and population. Once you find some Bulletin Board Systems you like, you'll see the comradery and entertainment a modem can bring to your life. (The free software alone is worth the price of a modem.)

Having a modem and some communications software for your computer can enhance your computer hobby in more ways than just meeting people over the phone lines. With a subscription to a commercial on-line service (kind of like a big, national BBS where you're billed for the time you spend on-line), you can shop, book airline tickets, advance your career, manage your money, play games, and more. In fact, no matter where your interests lie, a modem can make you wonder how you ever got along without one.

Do you long to play a good game of chess, but hate the trek over to your chess buddy's house across town? A modem and special modem gaming software for your computer lets you checkmate your opponent without seeing the sore loser's wrath in person. If chess or checkers aren't gory enough for you, many bestselling commercial computer games have begun offering the ability to play on-line (as long as your opponent also has a copy of the game software, along with a modem).

If you've always wanted to work at home, a modem and some remote access computer software can make this dream come true. These "remote control" packages give you the ability to control, monitor, and test software running on a PC somewhere else. You can transfer all your work files to your home computer from the comfort of home, and the donuts and coffee are handier.

We've all heard the computer experts predicting the day of the "paperless" office. But you'd probably like to see the day of the paperless home. This fantasy can be one step closer to reality with software that enables electronic banking. Imagine never having to write a paper check again—never mind messing with stamps, licking envelopes, and trying to find those freebie return address labels that charities are always sending you.

TASKS FOR MODEMS & TELECOMMUNICATIONS SOFTWARE

- Calling Bulletin Board Systems
- Joining Commercial On-line Services

- Playing Games by Modem
- Remote Computing, or Working From Home
- Banking From Home

Calling Bulletin Board Systems

There is a BBS (Bulletin Board System, or "board") for every personality and interest imaginable. A quick glance at any local computer magazine's BBS list reveals boards devoted to every type of computer hardware configuration, as well as to such diversities as finance, surfing, and even genealogy.

Meeting people "on-line" who think the way you do and are willing to communicate is often described as a sort of "high." But before you sit down and program every Bulletin Board System you see into your communication program's dialing directory, you should look for a program that can help you save money and time.

Many local BBSs carry Telephone Prefix Checker utility programs that tell which prefixes are long distance or toll calls. You won't find these programs listed in the back of this chapter, because they are written by telecommunication enthusiasts with a specific city's telephone prefixes in mind. The best place to find handy programs like these is on a BBS—since people who run BBSs naturally have an interest in telecommunications programs of all kinds. You can quickly download (get the BBS computer to send it to your computer) these programs because they're small.

Prefix checker utility programs ask for your home phone's prefix (or the phone from which you're modeming) and the prefix of the BBS you want to call. The checker instantly tells you where the Bulletin Board System is located and whether or not calling it will cost you anything. Even if you've lived in your city all your life, a program like this comes in handy for pinpointing unfamiliar prefixes. Most of these programs are quick and colorful. Best of all, you don't have to sit there with the White Pages in your lap, checking each number against the prefix chart.

These prefix checkers work at any stage in the calling process. Whether you're wondering whether to call a BBS, or you find yourself in the middle of BBS somewhere and decide that downloading that 320K graphics demo just isn't worth it (especially if you find out the BBS is in the outer reaches of your county), the prefix checker pops right up.

Once you find a BBS that isn't a toll call and call it up, you'll probably be asked to think of a password for future log-ons. Rather than jotting your secret password on the nearest scrap of paper—or worse, *not* jotting it down at all—use your computer's filing skills to keep track of things. (Note: Use a different password for each system you log onto. If a BBS's user list is broken into by malicious pranksters, you could experience great chaos and confusion, not only there but on every system you call.)

Most BBSs have some telecommunications utilities that print a form to help you remember what you did during a call to a BBS. Many of these have blanks where you can fill in the date and time you last called a BBS, the names of people with whom you exchanged messages, what you downloaded and uploaded, and password and user I.D. records—all jotted down in one place.

Some BBSs are distinctive. You can tell right away what kind of people inhabit the board and if you feel comfortable there.

Other BBSs are harder to figure: Either there isn't much happening, or you haven't put enough time into finding out. The same holds true for users too, and that's why the sysop of a BBS will often ask a new user to write an on-line letter telling a little about himself or herself before they can obtain an "account" there.

What you do or don't reveal in the letter will sometimes motivate the sysop to give you a higher or lower level of access on the BBS. Generally, the higher your access, the more time you can spend on-line. With higher access you'll be participating in more discussion areas and file directories and better games. It's best to be yourself in the letter. Don't be afraid to go into some detail about your life, interests, and goals. After all, it's the neighborly thing to do, and remember, you're there to meet people.

Nobody likes a slug, and sysops are no exception. That's why your access level increases with the number of discussions in which you participate. The number of programs you upload also counts big with sysops. A bulletin board's vitality is quickly drained when everybody who logs on just reads personal messages, downloads a couple of games, and logs off.

Once you find a system that appeals to you, try to participate fully in the main board and the various discussion forums (sometimes known as "conferences" or "sub-boards"). Upload articles you think others would enjoy reading. If you make your presence known, you just might be stimulated, challenged, or enlightened. But you have to put energy into on-line communications to get anything back.

Due to the monstrous proportions media-hype has given the on-line phenomenon, it's hard to remember that most of those bizarre BBS names on that list represent a variety of groups of people striving for communication. So have fun! The decisions about what modem or communications software to buy are just the beginning of the choices you'll make in the on-line world.

COMMERCIAL ON-LINE SERVICES

Commercial on-line services seem to sprout as fast as BBSs. And, as with BBSs, there are many flavors of commercial on-line services from which to choose. Most of them offer similar services, however, such as on-line shopping, travel reservations, news, weather, sports, discussion areas, software downloading, and games.

Socializing On-Line Is Fun

You can increase your social circle rapidly when you join a commercial on-line service. They all offer on-line communications centers, with fast, inexpensive means of communicating with business associates, friends old and new, and family. You can send letters, documents, or your latest recipe for peach melba fudge through whatever electronic messaging system the commercial on-line service happens to use. Some of the commercial on-line services offer electronic CB simulators. This feature can be an expensive waste of time or a novel experience, depending on how you look at it.

Money Matters

Banking and brokerage services, annual reports of major companies, business news, stock market quotes, and forums on everything from personal finance to investing in baseball cards are offered by most of the commercial on-line services. Some of the services actually let you buy, sell, and trade in the stock market 24 hours a day.

You can learn to handle money more wisely. There are services that let you calculate interest payments and mortgage schedules, balance your checkbook, and figure your net worth.

Improve Your Chances

With the help of a commercial on-line service you can access any sort of industry-related information. This can be a big asset in furthering your career. Forums are available for lawyers, entrepreneurs, journalists—you name it. Resumes and job opportunities are often listed in special areas. Now you can let the experts give you career tips and advice.

The vast array of databases offered by most commercial on-line services lets you quickly add current information to reports, proposals, and even term papers. The news features offered by the commercial on-line services guarantee that your data will never be stale or erroneous.

Educational Resources

Many of the commercial on-line services offer on-line editions of encyclopedias and other reference materials. Rather than getting stuck with a soon-to-be-outmoded set of encyclopedias, access current information on-line. The many reference areas and databases offered by these services are essential educational tools. You can pick up information in the various discussion areas, too.

Computer-related discussion areas are almost as numerous as types of computers. You can learn as much or as little about your particular setup as you want. Industry experts can be accessed through electronic messaging capabilities. In fact, most of the commercial on-line services offer forums hosted by the big software publishers, so you can complain right on-line about that obscure software manual. Computer publications like *Dr. Dobb's Journal* and *Computer Language* can be found on some of the bigger commercial on-line services, like CompuServe.

News, Weather, and Sports

Many of the commercial on-line services subscribe to the AP News and Sports wires, as well as various weather services and business news services. Or, there are smaller, more specialized commercial on-line services devoted only to weather, news, or sports.

Fun and Games

News of your favorite rock star is just a key away. The larger commercial on-line services offer news, reviews, and up-to-date dirt on the doings of the rich and famous. Some of the services even offer daily soap opera summaries.

If gaming is what you're after, you can play arcade space-war, word and trivia, or fantasy-adventure games. One drawback is that you're getting charged for every minute you spend on-line.

Discussion areas of the larger on-line services offer news of comic books, electronics, music, sci-fi, and other entertainment doings. Hobby forums are fun to explore as well. Joining a commercial on-line service can ensure hours of entertainment.

Health and Nutrition

The more general commercial on-line services offer health-oriented databases. Since experts belong to the discussion forums, you can obtain up-to-date guidance on diet, first aid, preventive medicine, and more. Some of the commercial on-line services even offer support groups centering around such areas as substance abuse and living with cancer.

Many discussion forums offered by the larger commercial on-line services focus on gourmet cooking and good restaurants.

Shop, but not 'Til You Drop

Shopping in a giant electronic mall can be yours, 24 hours a day, with a membership in one of the larger commercial on-line services. Many well-known retailers and manufacturers have set up shop on the commercial on-line services. Some of the services offer discount shopping as well. Now you too can have the UPS guy blazing a trail to your door—just like Wally Wang.

If travel is in the cards for you, you can shop airfares, hotels, and tours with the travel features offered by the larger commercial on-line services. Once you find a fare or hotel rate that suits your budget, you can access air schedules and make reservations. Tickets can be picked up at your local travel agent or received by mail.

Before an overseas journey, you can check with CompuServe's Department of State's Travel Advisory Service for information about international currencies, vaccination and visa requirements, and customs regulations.

How Much Does It Cost?

Specific costs for each commercial on-line service change too rapidly to mention here. The on-line services have similar pricing structures, however. You pay an initial membership fee ranging from $25 to $50 for the more general services. You're then billed for any time you spend on-line, roughly $6 to $15 an hour. Some of the services charge a small monthly fee after the first three months of membership. Any travel arrangements you make are billed to your credit card as well. Each on-line service is listed in the back of this chapter. They all have toll-free numbers, and they'll be happy to answer questions about current fees and services.

TELECOMMUNICATIONS SOFTWARE

Once you've bought a modem, you'll need telecommunications software. Most of the software programs have similar features. Describing the many individual communications software packages available for each operating system would be redundant. Instead, here's a list of features you should look for in a communications package.

Make sure your communications package is easily configurable to your particular modem speed (the speed at which the computer you want to call is running) and other variables you may want to alter from time to time. Rigid software is the last thing you need. You'll want the software to provide a dialing directory, too, where you can add all the numbers you call and get your computer to automatically dial and redial the numbers at the touch of a key.

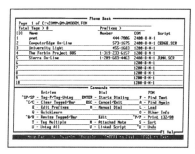

Figure 15: Typical of a dialing directory, QModem's *phone book lists BBSs you call frequently.*

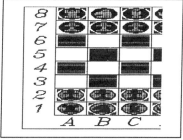

Figure 16: Play chess with a remote opponent with tele-gaming software.

A good communications program will offer a wide range of protocols for uploading and downloading files. Protocols are the actual file transfer programs that ensure your data is being transmitted in the most optimal method possible. *QModem SST* for the IBM/Compatible family of computers is superior in this area because it lets you add new, or "external," protocols as soon as they're developed. Since telecommunications programs and utilities are constantly being improved upon, being able to add new protocols is the best way to stay current. While on the subject of uploading and downloading files, make sure the process is easily accessible. Some programs let you upload or download in batches, allowing for the transfer of several files at one time.

You'll want to automate more than just the actual dialing and redialing process. Find a communications program that has a Quick Learn feature, so all your keystrokes on a particular BBS are memorized and a script, or giant macro, can be automatically generated. That way, next time you call, the script goes into effect automatically and you just kick back while your computer does all the work of logging in and joining conferences.

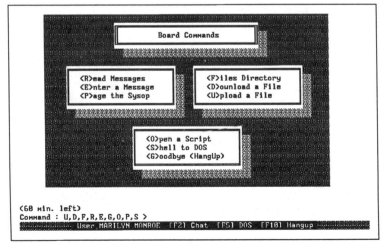

Figure 17: QModem's *host mode displays a menu to Folks calling your computer.*

You can take the automation process to the extreme by having the computer actually call the BBS by itself, log on, download all the mail waiting for you, upload any mail you want to send, and log off. This is great for calling BBSs in other cities when phone rates are cheapest. Top-notch programs have timer capabilities that make this feature easy. Other programs, such as the shareware IBM/Compatibles program called *The Brain*, are devoted only to this function. *The Brain* works by building a command file containing special commands the program enacts in your absence.

You may not use this next feature much as a beginner, but eventually you'll want other computers to be able to call yours. This is called "host mode," and most of the good shareware communications programs offer it. This lets you access your own computer from anywhere, or your friends can call your computer and upload that rad new EGA demo they've been raving about.

Make sure your communications program has a capture buffer, so you can save important messages or other information. Also, being able to access your disk operating system while in the communications software is important.

Finally, try to find a communications program with a good on-line help screen. Good shareware programs should come with a manual you can print out (be wary, though, the *QModem* manual has hundreds of pages and takes forever to print, and if you register the program and send a little extra, they'll mail you a nice, typeset manual).

GAMING WITH YOUR MODEM

It's 2025, violence has been outlawed, and the Sport of WAR, played by robots and based on the 20th Century game of football, is the most popular game in town. A modem version of the game has been developed for those with "a little concentration, a little dedication, and a lot of desire to pound your opponent into cube steak." So opens the futuristic manual to *Modem Wars*, a computer game with a twist.

Unlike most computer games, played in the solitude of your computer room, *Modem Wars* is played by two people. You compete on your computer via modem. The opponent is also hooked up to a computer and modem, but that opponent just may happen to be across town.

You don't even have to know your opponent. Many computer games are starting to offer modem play. Local Bulletin Board Systems usually offer lists of players specializing in different modem games. Once you access such a list, you can play against anybody equipped with a modem and a copy of the game.

Meet Grunt, Rider, Boomer, Spy, and Comcen, your robots to command. The press of a space bar determines which player picks the game type and map. Game types run the gamut from scrimmage (for beginners or those who just want to play quick and dirty) to full war. Look out! The full war game enables you to deploy your grunts (bombers) and missiles (anti-grunts).

A neat feature is the Voice/Pause option, which you get when you're playing the game over the phone lines. You can pick up the phone and talk with your opponent, and during the conversation the game will pause. This is handy when neither of you have read the manual and don't know what to do next.

The manual recommends that you find a player equal in skill to yours. You can figure your average game score and then handicap lesser players to even things out a bit.

You can send messages to your enemy any time by just hitting the return key. It's advisable to at least send a congratulatory message to the victor and a word of encouragement to the loser. Remarks like "Even my dog wouldn't do that" are not encouraged. Other games with modem play capabilities allow for on-line "chatting," or typing messages to each other, too.

On the more classical game front, another modem gaming software program features chess, checkers, and backgammon. *Teleplay* lets you sit down at the old cracker barrel for a rousing game of checkers, even if your opponent is miles away.

Teleplay is hard to play on an EGA screen because the chess pieces on the two sides are busy, and they're the same bright colors, just reversed. A plus is that you can send messages to your opponent, such as "What'd you do that for?" If things are really going badly, you can save the game for another day and go read up on what the great chessmasters would have done in your spot (of course, they never would have got into such a jam in the first place . . .).

WORKING FROM HOME

You can access your work computer at home with the help of remote computer software. Remote software runs in the background of both the local and remote computer until called up with hot keys. Both the remote and host computer can initiate calls using the dialing directory included with most of these packages. While connected, you can print files, transfer files, or show someone at the remote computer how to work a particularly difficult command. With the surge in popularity of laptop computers, imagine being able to control your PC back at the office from your hotel room. Family vacations will never be the same.

One of the most convenient features offered by most remote software packages is the ability to record screen sequences within a session for playback later. You can even pause within a session to play back earlier transactions. This is great for training and system troubleshooting.

BANKING FROM HOME

If banking is inconvenient, or you just want to partake of the ultimate that high-tech has to offer, you can pay bills electronically without ever setting pen to paper. When you write a paper check to a merchant, it makes its way back to the bank, where the amount is manually entered into a computer and transmitted to the Federal Reserve. With check writing programs, you enter and send your payment information directly to the Federal Reserve. Eliminate the middleman.

The plus is that it's safe, and the built-in check register keeps your account updated consistently. Tax time becomes a breeze. But there's always a minus—services like these are expensive.

COMMERCIAL ON-LINE SERVICES

- *Accu-Weather Forecaster*
  Accu-Weather, Metacomet Software, P.O. Box 31337
  Hartford, CT 06103, (800) 782-5661

- *AppleLink*
  Quantum Computer Services, Inc., 8619 Westwood Center Dr.
  Vienna, VA 22180

- *CompuServe Information Service*
  CompuServe, Inc., 5000 Arlington Centre Blvd.
  Columbus OH 43220, (614) 457-0802, (800) 848-8199

- *Connect Professional Information Network*
  Connect, Inc.1, 0101 Bubb Rd.
  Cupertino, CA 95014, (408) 973-0110, (800) 262-2638

- *DASnet Service*
  DA Systems, Inc., 1503 E. Campbell Ave.
  Campbell, CA 95008, (408) 559-7434

- *Dialog*
  Dialog Information Services, Inc., 3460 Hillview Ave.
  Palo Alto, CA 94304, (415) 858-2700, (800) 334-2564

- *Dow Jones News/Retrieval*
  Dow Jones & Company, Inc., P.O. Box 300
  Princeton, NJ 08543, (609) 520-4641

- *GEnie*
  General Electric Information Services, 401 N. Washington St.
  Rockville, MD 20850, (301) 340-4000, (800) 638-9636

- *Infomaster*
  InfoMaster, Dept. 520, 4230 Alpha Rd., Ste. 100
  Dallas, TX 75244, (800) 247-1373

- *Lexis/Nexis*
  Mead Data Central, 9443 Springsboro Pike, P.O. Box 933
  Dayton, OH 45401, (800) 227-4908

- *MCI Mail*
  MCI Mail, 1150 17th St. NW, 8th Fl.
  Washington, DC 20036, (202) 833-8484, (800) 444-6245

- *NewsNet, Inc.*
  NewsNet, Inc., 945 Haverford Rd.
  Bryn Mawr, PA 19010, (215) 527-8030, (800) 345-1301

- *PC-Link*
  Quantum Computer Services, Inc., 8619 Westwood Center Dr.
  Vienna, VA 22180

- *The Source*
  Source Telecomputing, 1616 Anderson Rd., P.O. Box 1305
  McLean, VA 22101, (703) 821-6666, (800) 336-3366

IBM/COMPATIBLES TELECOMMUNICATIONS SOFTWARE

- *Boyan 4.0*, $55.00
  Boyan Communications, 9458 Two Hills Court
  Columbia, MD 21045-3228
  (919) 682-4225 (BBS)

- *Crosstalk XVI* 3.7, $195.00
  DCA/Crosstalk Communications, 1000 Holcomb Woods Pkwy.
  Roswell, CA 30076, (404) 998-3998, (404) 998-8048 (BBS)

- *Crosstalk Mk. 4* 1.1, $245.00
  DCA/Crosstalk Communications, 1000 Holcomb Woods Pkwy.
  Roswell, CA 30076, (404) 998-3998
  (404) 641-1083 (BBS)

- *Freeway Advanced* 3.0, $139.00
  Kortek, Inc., 460 California Ave.
  Palo Alto, CA 94306, (800) 327-0310, 415) 327-4555

- *Mirror III* 1.0, $99.95
  SoftKlone Distributing Corp., 327 Office Plaza Dr., #100
  Tallahassee, FL 32301, (904) 878-8564
  (904) 878-9884 (BBS)

- *ProComm Plus* 1.1b, $89.00
  Datastorm Technologies, Inc., 3212 Lemonne Blvd.
  P.O. Box 1471, Columbia, MO 65201
  (314) 474-8461, (314) 474-8477 (BBS)

- *Qmodem SST* 4.0, $45.00 (manual $15.00)
  The Forbin Project, Inc., P.O. Box 702
  Cedar Falls, IA 50613, (319) 232-4516, (319) 233-6157 (BBS)

- *Relay Gold* 3.0, $295.00
  Microcom Software Division, 41 Kenosia Ave.
  Danbury, CT 06810-9990, (800) 847-3529, (203) 798-3800

- *Smartcomm III* 1.1a, $249.00
  Hayes Microcomputer Products, Inc., P.O. Box 105203
  Atlanta, GA 30348, (404) 441-1617
  (800) 847-2937 (BBS)

- *The Brain* (Disk #752)
  PC-SIG, 1030 East Duane Avenue, Ste. D
  Sunnyvale, CA 94086, (800) 222-2996 (CA)
  (800) 245-6717 (USA), (408) 730-9291

IBM/COMPATIBLE CONNECTIVITY SOFTWARE

- *Laplink Plus*, $139.95
  File transfer software (IBM compatible desktops and laptops)
  Traveling Software, Inc., 18702 North Creek Parkway
  Bothell, WA 98011 (800) 343-8080

MACINTOSH COMMUNICATIONS SOFTWARE

- *MicroPhone II*, $295.00
  Telecommunications (Macintosh 512KE or larger)
  Software Ventures Corp., 2907 Claremont Ave., Ste. 220
  Berkeley, CA 94705 (800) 336-6477

- *Red Ryder*, $80.00
  Telecommunications (Macintosh 512K and larger)
  FreeSoft, 150 Hickory Dr.
  Beaver Falls, PA 15010 (412) 846-2700

- *Smartcom II* for the Mac, $149.00
  Terminal emulation (Any Macintosh)
  Hayes Microcomputer Products, Inc., PO Box 105203
  Atlanta, GA 30348 (404) 449-8791

- *Quick Link II*, $99.00
  Telecommunications (Mac 512K and larger)
  Smith Micro Software, Inc., PO Box 7137
  Huntington Beach, CA 92615 (714) 964-0412

CONNECTIVITY SOFTWARE

- *MacBlast*, $195.00
  Asynchronous file transfer software (Mac Plus or larger)
  Communications Research Group, 5615 Corporate Blvd.
  Baton Rouge, LA 70808 (504) 923-0888
  or (800) 242-5278

- *MacLinkPlus*, $200.00
  File tranfer and translation software
  (Macintosh Plus or larger)
  Data Viz, Inc., 35 Corporate Dr.
  Trumbull, CT 06611 203-268-0030

- *ProLink*, $59.95
  File transfer software (Apple II and Macintosh)
  Alsoft, Inc., PO Box 927
  Spring, TX 77383 (713) 353-4090

MODEM GAMING SOFTWARE

- *Modem Wars*, $39.95
  Electronic Arts, P.O. Box 7578
  San Mateo, CA 94403-7578, (415) 572-2787

- *TelePlay*, $19.95
  Teletronics, Inc., 3368 Govenor Dr., Ste. F-252
  San Diego, CA 92122

REMOTE ACCESS SOFTWARE

- *Carbon Copy plus*, $195.00
  Microcom, 500 River Ridge Dr.
  Norwood, MA 02062-5028, (617) 551-1999

- *pcAnywhere III*, $140.00 (IBM/Compatibles)
  Dynamic Microprocessor Associates, Inc., 60 E. 42nd St.
  NY, NY 10165

MODEM BANKING SOFTWARE

- *CheckFree*, $49.95 (IBM/Compatibles)
  CheckFree Technologies, P/O. Box 897
  Colombus, OH 43216, (614) 898-6000

APPENDIX A

Shareware Isn't Scareware

Most shareware and public domain programs discussed in this book come on a single diskette, without any fancy packaging or manuals. This is a mixed blessing. These no-frills programs can be distributed cheaply (or for free, in the case of public domain software). On the other hand, some people feel intimidated without manuals and packaging to assist them in becoming familiar with the software.

No need for alarm. It's easy to get up and running with a new shareware diskette. Simply insert the diskette into your floppy drive (probably Drive A), change to drive a:, and type "dir" to get a directory of the diskette's contents. (Note: If the program is large, and the diskette's contents scroll by while you watch helplessly, type "dir/p" instead. That will give you the directory a Page at a time. Another directory favorite is "dir/w" which gives you a Wide, or horizontal directory—taking up less space while letting you see everything at once. This last is recommended for DOS gurus only, since the display doesn't clearly differentiate between filenames and subdirectories.)

By now you've typed "dir" and the contents of the shareware diskette are up there on the screen. It's easy to tell what the files in the program do—just look at their extensions. Extensions are those three letters that come after the period in a filename. For example, in a file named wp.exe, the extension is "exe." Following is a list of the most common, and important, extensions and what they do.

FILE EXTENSIONS AND THEIR FUNCTIONS

.EXE
This stands for "executable" file and runs the program. Type what comes before .exe and press the enter key; the program should start up. For example, if the filename were Baseball.exe, type "Baseball" at the prompt and the program will start running.

.COM
This stands for "command" file, and will run the program. Type what comes before .com, press the enter key, and the program should run.

.BAT
This stands for "batch" file, which someone has written to make starting up the program or printing documentation easier. Type what comes before .bat and press the enter key.

.BAS
This stands for "BASIC" and you must be in the BASIC program that came with your computer in order to run a program with this extension.

.DOC, OR .TXT
These stand for documentation files, and you may access this important information in two ways. Either type "type whatever.doc" (in which case you have to keep pressing "Ctrl-S" to get it to stop scrolling down your screen so quickly you can't

read it). Or you can type "list whatever.doc" if you have the handy utility "List" on your hard drive. Be sure to read the .doc or .txt file *before* running the program.

.READ.ME

If you see any variation of this filename on the program diskette, first type "type read.me" or "list read.me" (if you have the "List" utility mentioned above), before doing anything else—especially trying to run the actual program. Chances are this file contains last-minute information crucial to getting the program running.

.ARC

This stands for "archived" file and means that the entire program is hiding in here with all of its various files compressed, or archived, into one neat package. (Computer programmers are into neatness.) The diskette probably contains a de-compression or unarchiving utility, probably called pkxarc.com or pkunpak.ctl. If these programs are there, to unarchive the program, stick a blank, formatted diskette in your b: drive, and type "pkxarc program b:" (substitute the actual filename for the word "program" here). Magically, the program will decompress onto the diskette in drive b:, and instead of one big file you'll have several. If you have a hard disk, it's recommended to make a special subdirectory there just for unarchiving and trying out new shareware programs. I call mine "junk." That way, I can type "pkxarc program c:\junk," and all the programs files go obediently to junk, where they're easy to identify and keep separate from the other programs on my hard disk. And if I don't like the program, I just type del c:\junk *.* and it's gone.

Of course, you'll see many other file extensions on program diskettes, but these are the basics and ought to get you going.

APPENDIX B

The World of CD-ROM

Imagine a pile of 1,484 floppy disks, packed full of 10,000 neat, offbeat, useful shareware applications. Wouldn't it be fun to have all those disks and programs at once? Think of all the interesting hobby and household applications hiding in these disks. Storing and accessing them all could be a mess, though, unless you're a supremely organized being.

Now, imagine being able to keep all those programs on your computer, ready for use at the press of a key. Sound impossible? The marvels of computer compact disk technology, or CD-ROM, make accessing any program quick and easy.

The real advantage to having CD-ROM (Compact Disk-Read Only Memory) is that CD-ROM discs are able to store much more information than floppy or even hard disks. So, although you can only read off them and not write information to them (as the name Read-Only Memory implies), a typical CD-ROM disc can hold about 550 megabytes, or the equivalent of about 1,565 of the older 360K MS-DOS diskettes, 700 of the newer, double-sided 3 1/2-inch diskettes, or ten 55MB hard disks. Think of CD-ROM discs as a kind of publishing medium, but one where the information is in a computer-readable form ready to be copied over into any of your normal applications. (And, a CD-ROM disc is easier than 1,565 diskettes to tuck in your pocket.)

WHAT'S AVAILABLE ON CD-ROM MEDIA?

At first, commercial CD-ROM discs focused on information useful mostly to corporations, financial whizzes, and libraries. CD-ROM discs can easily handle huge databases, since they have such large capacities. But now, more and more publishers are putting out CD-ROM discs of interest to the home user. There's even a magazine devoted solely to new CD-ROM products and developments: *CD-ROM Review*.

Microsoft *Bookshelf*

Crowded onto one CD-ROM disc are all the programs a student or writer could ever want. *Bookshelf* features *The American Heritage Dictionary*, *Roget's II Electronic Thesaurus*, *Bartlett's Familiar Quotations*, the *Chicago Manual of Style*, the *Houghton Mifflin Spelling Verifier and Corrector*, the *Houghton Mifflin Usage Alert*, *The World Almanac and Book of Facts* (for the current year), the *U.S. Zip Code Directory*, *Business Information Sources*, and a collection of business and personal forms and letters.

Bookshelf's most attractive feature is that it's RAM resident, so it can pop up in the middle of your favorite word processor or other application. I enjoyed typing an address in a *WordPerfect* letter, pressing a key, and seeing *Bookshelf* zap in the zip code.

The PC-SIG Library on CD-ROM

Wow! The *PC-SIG Library on CD-ROM* disc is stuffed with every single shareware and public domain program distributed by the folks at PC-SIG, the Silicon Valley company who pioneered the concept of shareware in the early days of the PC and who keep the world's largest library of shareware programs. (See Appendix One for a discussion of shareware.)

With this disc, you can access, copy to a hard disk or a floppy, and run powerful business programs, personal productivity tools, educational programs, programming tools, home software you've seen mentioned in other chapters in this book, games, and even desktop publishing software.

A plus: The CD-ROM disc comes with a 432-page book, *The Encyclopedia of Shareware*, so you can browse in bed and decide which programs to play with next.

Oxford English Dictionary

Did you ever get suckered into joining the Book of the Month Club just so you could buy the compact edition of the *Oxford English Dictionary* (*OED*) for $25 instead of $250? Did you regret ordering it once you found out you had to use a magnifying glass to read it? Here's where CD-ROM technology really shines.

Available in a two-disc set, the CD-ROM *Oxford English Dictionary* lets you call up any word, whether obscure or everyday (talk about in-depth: this dictionary devotes seven pages to the word "what"). You can simply find out what it means or read further to learn the word's origin. The best feature of the *OED* is that each entry contains several passages showing how the word's usage has evolved through the ages. If the word really intrigues you, you can even trace related or opposite words. Best of all, you can copy any passage into whatever document you want.

The Electronic Whole Earth Catalog

You may or may not be familiar with the *Whole Earth Catalog*, a book listing resources on almost every field of interest under the sun, first published in 1968 by Stewart Brand. When it first came out, the book was hailed by counter-culture types for its democratic and "you can do anything yourself" attitude.

The latest book version weighs over 5 1/2 pounds, so the publishers decided to offer the catalog in electronic form (for Macintosh computers). The CD-ROM resource contains more than 3,500 entries on many subjects—from building your own home, managing and operating a small business, beekeeping, blacksmithing, your body and your well-being—even computers.

Better than a book, the CD-ROM disc features cross-referencing, sound, and visuals. For example, users can actually listen to excerpts from more than 700 recordings, from blues to jazz to bird calls. Full-screen digitized images and more than 3,000 graphics are included, as well.

WHAT YOU NEED TO GET STARTED WITH CD-ROM

The components of a CD-ROM setup include the CD-ROM disc, a CD-ROM drive unit, a disc caddie, a controller card, a cable, and a few manuals. And, of course, your computer.

The CD-ROM Disc, or Software

First of all, you'll need a CD-ROM disc. Find a disc on a topic or field of interest to you, because at $295-plus, the CD-ROM disc you choose should last awhile.

The CD-ROM Drive, or Hardware

The primary piece of hardware needed to "play" a CD-ROM disc is a CD-ROM drive. CD-ROM drives come in both external and internal forms, just like modems. Because they cost so much more than any other computer accessory, however, your best bet is to buy an external CD-ROM drive. That way, you don't have to worry about incompatibility in case you ever want to buy a new computer from a different computer family. If, for example, you decided to switch from a Macintosh computer to an IBM/compatible, you'd only have to replace the CD-ROM drive's controller card and cable—much less expensive than replacing the whole drive unit.

The external CD-ROM drive looks like a half-height computer box, but in place of a floppy disk drive there's a CD-ROM slot. Don't stick the CD-ROM disc right into the slot, however. Instead, slip the disc carefully into the removable disc caddie included with the drive. Then close the caddie and push it part way into the drive's slot, which grabs it and automatically inserts the caddie the rest of the way into the slot. When you want to quit your CD-ROM session, just press the eject button under the slot, and the disc caddie pops out, ready to be loaded with another disc.

Included with the external CD-ROM drive is a CD-ROM controller card, which fits into an empty slot in your computer. Once it's snapped into place, a cable connects the controller card in your computer to the CD-ROM drive. It's important to make sure you have the correct interface cable for both the controller card and your model of CD-ROM drive. The CD-ROM drive also comes with an AC power cord, ready to take up yet another slot on your computer's power strip.

Now all the hardware is in place. But one crucial aspect is still missing. Your computer needs software to tell it there's a CD-ROM drive hooked up to it. (You'd think the computer would notice this intruder on its own, but it doesn't.)

This software varies, depending on what type of computer you own. The CD-ROM software for IBM/Compatible computers is published by Microsoft. It's called "MS-DOS CD-ROM Extensions." For the Macintosh family of computers, an INIT file comes with the CD-ROM hardware and this tells the Mac to treat the CD-ROM drive like any other disk drive.

If you have an IBM/Compatible computer, you'll probably need to add lines in your computer's config.sys and autoexec.bat files, telling your computer to look for the alien drive each time it boots up. The manuals and other user documentation that come with the drive and individual discs are very thorough, however, so you shouldn't have any trouble if you read these carefully before attempting installation.

SOURCES FOR CD-ROM PRODUCTS

- *CD-ROM Review*, $35.00/year
  CW Communications/Peterborough, P.O. Box 921
  Farmingdale, NY 11737-9621

- *Bookshelf*, $250.00
  Microsoft Corporation, 16011 NE 36th Way, P.O. Box 97017
  Redmond WA 98073-9717, (206) 882-8080

- *PC-SIG CD-ROM*, $149.00
  PC-SIG, 1030 East Duane Avenue, Ste. D
  Sunnyvale, CA 94086, (800) 222-2996 (CA)
  (800) 245-6717 (USA), (408) 730-9291

- Educorp Macintosh Shareware CD-ROM, $199.00
  531 Stevens Ave., Ste. B
  Solana Beach, CA 92075, (800) 843-9497, (619) 259-0255

- *Oxford English Dictionary*, $1250.00
  TriStar Publishing, 475 Virginia Drive
  Fort Washington, PA 19034, (215) 641-9600

- *The Electronic Whole Earth Catalog*, $149.95
  Broderbund Software, Inc., 17 Paul Drive
  San Rafael, Ca 94903-2101, (415) 492-3200

- The Sony Corporation
  2132A East Dominguez St.
  Carson, CA 90810

- Amdek Corp.
  3471 North First St. Bldg. #3
  San Jose, CA 95134, (408) 436-8570

Index

Other computer books from
Computer Publishing Enterprises:

How to Understand and Buy Computers
By Dan Gookin

Parent's Guide to Educational Software and Computers
by Lynn Stewart and Toni Michael

How to Understand and Find Software
by Wally Wang

How to Get Started With Modems
by Jim Kimble

The Best FREE Time-Saving Utilities for the PC
by Wally Wang

101 Computer Business Ideas
by Wally Wang

How to Start a Business With a Computer
by Jack Dunning